MANAGING
STRESS

MANAGING STRESS

STRESS

A Creative Journal

Brian Luke Seaward, Ph.D.

Department of Health and Fitness
The American University
Washington, D.C.

Jones and Bartlett Publishers

Boston   London

Editorial, Sales and Customer Service Offices
Jones and Bartlett Publishers
One Exeter Plaza
Boston, MA 02116
1-800-832-0034
617-859-3900

Jones and Bartlett Publishers International
P.O. Box 1498
London W6 7RS
England

Library of Congress Cataloging-in-Publication Data

Seaward, Brian Luke.
  Managing stress: a creative journal/ Brian Luke Seaward.
  p.   cm.
  Includes bibliographical references.
  ISBN 0–86720–841–4
  1. Stress Management. 2. Diaries — Therapeutic use. 3. Diaries —
Authorship. I. Title.
  RA785.S433   1994
  155.9' 042—dc20   93-40223
                                                                CIP

Credits: p.xv, 25 Sam Campagna; p. 1 Diana Dee Tyler, Three Bears Heads © copyright 1981. Reprinted with permission; pp. 3, 16, 21, 27, 30, 46 Roger Navis; p. 5 Copyright 1984 ZIGGY and Friends, Inc. Distributed by Universal Press Syndicate. Reprinted with permission. All rights reserved; pp. 8, 48, 80 Gail Seaward Wall; pp. 19, 23, 39, 40 Racquel Keller; p. 38 VIP © copyright, Redwing Shoes. Reprinted with permission. All photographs are courtesy of the author.

Printed in the United States of America
98 97 96 95 94 10 9 8 7 6 5 4 3 2 1

*This workbook is dedicated to
my sister, Gail, who has slayed many personal dragons
with a pen and paper.*

By the power of the written word to make you hear,
to make you feel... before all, to make you see.
That, and no more, and it is everything.

—Joseph Conrad, on writing

CONTENTS

ACKNOWLEDGMENTS

This workbook has seen many incarnations, most notably in the past five years under the title of *My Best Friend: A Creative Journal for Stress Management*. I am most grateful to Jones and Bartlett Publishers for their interest in publishing this in conjunction with *Managing Stress: Principles and Strategies for Health and Wellbeing*. There are several people I would like to thank for nurturing this project throughout the years. To Joe Burns, Paula Carroll, Mary Cervantes, and Amina Sharma at Jones and Bartlett, thanks for your assistance in the publication of this workbook. To Paige Erikson and Michael Dalrymple, thank you so much for your tutorials on the Macintosh; I owe you both another dinner. To Lonnie Dalrymple, thanks for being another set of eyes — all sorrows *can* be borne, right? To Diana Dee Tyler, whom over the years I have most affectionately called "The Bear Lady," thank you for giving me permission to use your wonderful piece of art work: *Three Bears Heads*. To my agent, Debbie Kitchen, thanks for your support in this project in its earlier life; there's more to come, I promise! To my sister, Gail, and my dear friends Roger Navis, Racquel Keller, and Sam Campagna, thank you so much for your artwork which enhances these pages, bringing the journal themes to life. To my mentors and colleagues who have served as a great inspiration on my own path of enlightenment: Elisabeth Kubler-Ross, Roger von Oech, Patricia Norris, Larry Dossey, Joan Borysenko, Bernie Siegel, and Jean Shinoda Bolen, to name just a few. And finally, thanks to my support network, Bonnie Moore, Mary Jane Mees, Skylar Sherman, Rob Sleamaker, Neal and Rita Carlson, Linda Campanelli, Susan Moran, Ingrid Helvig, Andy Frank, Betsy Meholick, Mark Ricard, Doug Backland, Dan and Michelle Parent, Anne Cassels-Brown, Jeanne Plo, Jack Dobek, Laurie Caswell, Craig Broaderdorp, Steve Fitzgerald for your inspiration and friendship, and all my students at The American University, who have been wonderful teachers in their own right.

INTRODUCTION
The Importance of Journal Writing

"All sorrows can be borne, if you put them in a story."
—Isak Dinesen

At the turn of the twentieth century, British East Africa, now know as Kenya, was a land ripe with adventure, from Mount Kilimanjaro to the Serengeti Plain. It attracted many an expatriate from the shores of Europe, Asia, and the Americas. Among these new citizens was the Dane Karen Blixen, the new wife of Baron Von Blixen, who settled down to carve a future life at the foot of the Ngong Hills, just outside Nairobi. A life of high adventure is not without its stressful episodes. In her seventeen years spent in Africa, Karen contracted syphilis from an unfaithful husband, severed her relationship with the Baron, and lost her farm to fire and her land to bankruptcy. Perhaps worst of all was when she lost the one man she loved, Denys Finch Hatton, in the crash of a Gypsy Moth two-seater plane.

Throughout her life in Africa, Karen wrote. Writing and storytelling became a release, almost an escape; but in every case they were a means to cope with the changes that she encountered. Upon what she called an ungraceful return to her home in Denmark, Karen began to compose and organize the memories of her African adventures. The result was a wonderful collection of personal experiences intertwining the sad with the sublime, written under the pen name Isak Dinesen, to become the classic novel *Out of Africa*. While not everyone is a novelist, we all have life adventures that merit, often necessitate, a vehicle of expression— an expression that helps to ease the pain of the soul. In the words of Karen Blixen, "All sorrows can be borne, if you put them in a story."

To open up, share, and disclose feelings, perceptions, opinions, and memories has always been found to be therapeutic. Confessions of the mind can lighten the burden of the soul. Many religions have adapted this concept for spiritual healing. This is also the cornerstone upon which modern psychotherapy is based. Although conversation is the most common method of disclosure, writing down thoughts that occupy the mind is extremely therapeutic as well. Journal writing can be defined as a series of written passages that document the personal events, thoughts, feelings, memories, and perceptions in the journey throughout one's life leading to wholeness. Journal writing has proven to be a formidable coping technique to deal with stress, so much so that for years, psychologists and health educators alike have used journal writing as an awareness tool for self-exploration and enhancing personal development.

Often, there comes a time when our minds get overloaded with sensory stimulation and it seems that we cannot think straight. This is part of the "stress response"— unclear thinking due to sensory overload. The repercussions, including unfocused judgments, poor perspective, bad decision making, and eventual poor health, are dangerous. The cycle can become so strong that it never breaks. Actually, stress goes deeper than this. We live in an age where we hardly know ourselves at a profound level. We just don't take the time to examine our thoughts, feelings, perceptions and attitudes. Not being honest with our true feelings leaves us empty handed when we face life's daily stressors. In a world where change is perhaps the only constant factor, we continually need to stay in close touch with our thoughts, feelings, and perceptions to guide us through or around life's obstacles.

How does a journal fit in? The word *journal* comes from the root word *journee* meaning a day's travel, or to journey or travel. Journals originally started as a means of guidance on long trips, an orientation record for a safe return passage. From Columbus to Lewis and Clark to today's astronauts, journal writing has been and continues to be a proven means of personal guidance on each individual's journey through life. When pen or pencil is taken in hand and put to paper, a connection is made between the mind and the soul. Thoughts that are written down on paper make the author accountable for those thoughts. These thoughts become real, tangible, and focused, they become concrete. By taking the time to write down the thoughts and feelings that congest or trouble your mind, you develop a habit of clearing your mind of concerns, problems, and issues that constantly demand your attention. Unloading one's thoughts can help clean the conscious mind. It also helps to initiate the resolution process in dealing with life's stressors. When personal issues are written down, not only is there a cathartic effect, but often insight into the resolution of these problems begins to unfold.

How does journal writing relate to stress management? Quite simply, the best stress management program deals with both the causes and symptoms of stress. Relaxation techniques are great for dealing effectively with the signs and symptoms of stress (e.g., ulcers, migraines, hypertension, etc.). If, however, you only give attention to the symptoms of stress, and not the causes of the perceived tension, then relaxation techniques are only a temporary solution to a chronic problem. The best way to deal with the cause of your stress is to first increase your awareness of what your stressors are. What is it that really bothers you? You cannot put strategies into action if the real cause of your problems is fogged in within the depths of your mind.

Journal writing opens the doors to your conscious mind and allows you to really examine what you are feeling—where you have traveled in the course of a day, and where this journey has taken you with your own mental, emotional, and spiritual growth and development. By writing in your journal for a period of weeks or months, and then reading through these passages of your life's journey, you will begin to see specific patterns to your thinking, your emotional responses, and even your actions and behaviors; patterns that are unnoticeable on a day-to-day basis. This is where the real self-learning process takes place. From this ability to see patterns in your thoughts and behaviors, you can get a better bearing on how to deal with the issues and concerns that cause stress. Current research suggests that not only is journal writing good for the soul, but it is also good for the body. Studies by James Pennebaker, in which individuals kept journals and wrote about their frustrations and painful experiences, revealed that, over time, they had fewer physical ailments (e.g., headaches, cramps, colds, etc.) suggesting a new bond in the link between mind and body.

The idea for this journal workbook came from a series of homework assignments that I gave to my students as exercises in self-awareness to deal with perceived stress. Actually, the origins for these assignments came from a workshop I attended several years ago on self-reflection. One of the workshop experiences, based on a book by Anne Morrow Lindbergh entitled *Gift from the Sea*, involved selecting a sea shell from a basket loaded with all kinds of objects from the ocean floor. The shell then served as a tool for introspection; by centering, focusing and touching the shell we could focus and get in touch with ourselves. Although there was no writing involved, I liked the idea so much that I adapted it for my own stress management class as an in-class journal assignment. It became an instant hit. Other journal themes then followed.

Since then I have searched for other similar experiences and have included these in the workbook as well. With particular interest I share the theme of the Vision Quest. On a recent trip back home to Colorado, I discovered the Native American tradition of the Vision Quest. I found it to be a very moving experience, and this too I adapted for the workbook. As an in-class journal assignment, it also has become quite popular because it also reaches to the depths of one's soul. Other assignments were inspired from a great many books I have read (see References section listed at the back of the workbook for further reading on self-discovery). Generally, I have found that, depending on where each person is in his or her life journey, certain journal themes hold greater significance. I have tried to create an assortment of topics, issues, and concerns that I have experienced in my own life as well as those I have encountered through the lives of my students, clients, and workshop participants.

At first, journal writing can seem tedious and difficult. This often occurs because we are not in the habit of articulating our innermost feelings. But after a while, like any skill, you become better at it. Included are many suggested journal theme entries to help you get started with this process to enhance your journal writing and self-awareness skills. These theme entries serve to motivate and maintain the writing process. They were created to serve as catalysts for soul searching as well as to give you a jump start when you need writing motivation. You are, however, strongly encouraged to write on your own, with no other theme than "what's on your mind today?" There is no particular order to the selected journal themes. Although these subjects are outlined in the table of contents, you may begin with any journal theme, or simply write on anything that you feel is important and merits your attention. It is important to remember that when you write, write of yourself and for yourself, not to others or for others. The contents of this journal aren't for publication. They are confidential (unless perhaps, they are assigned for a class or workshop). Your thoughts should be articulated, yet unedited. When you begin to accept this premise, your writing becomes much easier and more honest, and the rewards are more fruitful.

When is the best time to write? This varies from person to person. The end of the day is often an ideal time, but perhaps this is not convenient given your schedule. You really have to decide for yourself. Journal writing time, however, should be uninter-rupted time, quality alone time. How often should you take pen in hand and write? It is suggested that the benefits of journal writing are realized when there is continuity with journal entries. A good goal to start with is a minimum of three entries per week. Moreover, journal entries don't always have to be filled with thoughts and descriptions of stressful events based on fear or anger. They can recount good times as well. Life is a combination of positive and negative experiences and your journal should reflect this. Mostly, by keeping a regular habit of journal writing you really begin to know yourself well, and eventually, in the process, become your own best friend.

Best wishes and inner peace,
BLS

JOURNAL SUMMARY EXCERPTS

The following are some excerpts from journal summaries that I have come across in my several years of teaching college students and journal writing workshops. These might serve as an inspiration to keep a journal on a regular basis.

"The journal helped me to identify what my values are. I found that my values are somewhat different than I had originally thought. I always made the assumption that my beliefs were the same as those of my parents. Although there is some validity to this, there are some areas where my values differ from theirs. Through the use of my journal, I learned how important value definition is in how I perceive things. The last trend that I noticed in my journal was the increasing number and effectiveness of my options for reducing stress. At the beginning, I didn't have any; but as time went on, I came up with better options. I took this to mean that I was learning something—I hope so."

"For a long time now, I've known what stresses me the most. It has been a long time since I've been able to confide in or let anyone get really close to me. I've been so wrapped up in school for the past eight years of my life, and it's really getting lonely. As time goes on, it gets harder and harder to express myself. In a sense, I'm scared of situations because I don't know how I'll react. In this aspect I don't know myself very well and I'm afraid to find out. This journal has really helped me get in touch with myself."

"This stress reduction journal offered no cure-all for my problems, but it gave me valuable help. It helped me understand and see what I thought. By knowing what was going through my mind, I began to realize things about myself, some things I might have never known. A common phrase I saw within my journal was 'good enough.' The paper was 'good enough,' the letter I wrote home was 'good enough,' I was doing things so they would be 'good enough' and in doing so, not achieving my potential. I was striving for mediocrity. I'm trying to break this bad habit and I think I have made a little headway. Creativity is now more clear and interesting to me than ever before. I found myself writing short stories in my journal or just creating ideas for work or pleasure."

"When I divorced my husband of seven years, I cried on everyone's shoulder for months. That was a year ago. But people get tired of the same old complaints, even your best friends. So I took refuge in writing in my journal. It served as a great sounding board. It certainly helped me heal some very deep wounds. I've learned that there are some thoughts that are best left between my mind and the pages of a journal notebook."

"Toxic thoughts! I didn't know I harbored so many of these. I really thought I held an optimistic attitude, but I saw that there is a strong correlation between certain negative attitudes and their corresponding stressors. When the thoughts find their way

on paper, they tend to lose their toxic effects in my body. Over the past three months I've seen some things in myself that I often dislike in others. Humm! Very therapeutic. By the way, there were a lot of good times I was reminded of and I'm glad that I have some details to fall back on on occasion. I even found myself laughing out loud."

"Things have always bugged me, but I was never sure what. The journal helped me realize that several things really bugged me and led me to a way to solve my problems. This may sound trivial, but it used to cause me no end of pain. When someone is bothering me and that person asked me 'What's wrong?' I always answer, 'Nothing.' I automatically think they should know what is wrong, but I am wrong in thinking this. I have learned that it bugs me to not tell people they are bothering me. This may seem like a trivial point but I found it a very interesting realization."

"Keeping a journal has revealed that I am insecure and unsure about a great many things that I have been putting a false facade on to cover up these feelings. I sometimes think too much, and I often don't think at all. This emotional predicament may cause other people trouble, but I am beginning to take some comfort in my humanness. I look at it this way; someone once said, 'Poetry is mass confusion understood.' At times my mind is mass confusion. Through my journal if I can begin to understand it, I'll be poetry in motion."

LONGS PEAK, COLORADO

JOURNAL THEMES

1. TOP TEN STRESSORS

There are many surveys and questionnaires to help people identify circumstances that cause stress and the intensity of frustration that they create. But these questionnaires can be quite impersonal and, typically, they tell us what we already know–that indeed we do have stress. But often times people are not aware of what the cause of their stress is because they don't take the time to examine it. More often than not, people usually ignore or avoid their stressors, hoping they will go away. Seldom, if ever, does this approach work and usually these problems don't go away. In fact, they usually haunt us until we take some positive action.

The best way to start to get a handle on the cause of your stress is to pinpoint exactly what is bothering you. By writing down what is on your mind you begin to get a better idea of what it's all about. So take a moment to think about what is on your mind, what is troubling you, or what caused you to get angry or afraid of something lately. Make a list and then prioritize your top ten stressors from the most stressful to the least stressful. If you have fewer than ten, fine. Don't feel compelled to add more than you really have. Once you have made this list, describe each stressor in a couple of sentences so you have a really good focus on each one.

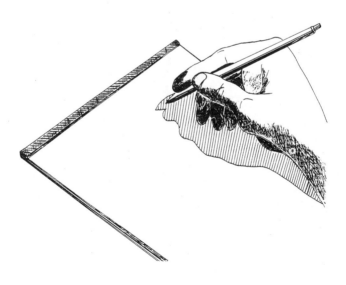

3

2. WHO AM I?

Who am I? This is, perhaps, the hardest question we will ever encounter in the course of our life. We wear many hats, play many roles, and wear many faces, sometimes all in the course of one day. If our environment were constant throughout life, the answer might seem easier, but we live in a dynamic world where change is constant. Some would advocate that we are our current identity, while others might say that we are a collection of all our experiences. Perhaps the truth lies somewhere in between.

Take a moment to think about who and all that you really are. What roles do you play (student, roommate, son, daughter, mother, father, colleague, confidant, supervisor, neighbor, spouse, brother, sister, friend) and what is the major role(s)? What makes up your current identity, what do you identify or associate yourself with, and what are the most significant experiences (good, bad, or ugly) that have contributed to your own make-up? Then articulate your thoughts on paper. Because change is constant, your answer today will most likely be different than your answer yesterday, or tomorrow. But by gaining a handle on who and all that we are, we can place ourselves in a grand self-perspective, to see the whole rather than fragmented pieces that distort this self-perspective. With a clear focus on who we are, we often gain a better handle on the challenges and concerns that enter our lives with this constant change in our world.

Who are you?

4

3. OPTIMIST OR PESSIMIST?

Some people are optimists and some are pessimists. Many people fall somewhere in between. In your opinion, describe the difference between an optimist and a pessimist, and give an example of each. Then explain which side you see yourself on most of the time and why.

4. HOW WAS YOUR DAY TODAY?

"How was your day today?" This is a standard question that wives, husbands, parents, children, or any loved ones pose to the working force as they return home from the office, dock, school, factory, or road. Now it is time to ask yourself. To sum up your day is a way to unload your mind from sensory overload as well as to help you identify and come to terms with the major issues and concerns experienced in the course of your day.

So, how was your day? Good or bad? Did any significant events (positive or negative) occur? How do you feel about them?

5. VISION QUEST

Our lives are a series of events strung together through the spirit of each breath and heartbeat. Some events are more significant than others, as they mark powerful changes in the growth and development of our existence. In earlier cultures as far back as the dawn of humankind, these events of change, these transitions from one life stage to another, were referred to as *rites of passage*. These rites often included a ceremony of celebration. Today, these are often continued in practices including bar mitzvahs, weddings, baby showers, and funerals.

In modern American culture, the importance of personal rites of passage has been de-emphasized or forgotten. Attention is placed on the ceremony without true recognition of its purpose. In reality, many of our major life events are done alone with no supportive guidance, no community involvement, and no celebration. Modern technology has also replaced our sense of origin, leaving us uncentered and ungrounded. The result often leaves us unable to deal effectively with the stress produced from life's crises or without the maturity to advance progressively through the developmental stages of life.

In the tradition of the native American Indian, a Vision Quest marks a significant rite of passage. It is a wilderness retreat where one reflects on one's inner resources as well as reaffirms one's centeredness and connection to the Mother Earth. In a Vision Quest, the individual seeks a vision of a meaningful purpose in life and gains a greater understanding of oneself from within. This concept has been adopted as a cornerstone to the nation's Outward Bound program; self-reliance through introspection in nature. A Vision Quest marks a major life transition. Those who initiate this quest search for a vision to guide them through the transition period of change. Although in the truest sense, a Vision Quest is done in the solitude of the wilderness, you can initiate this process anywhere. The following questions are provided to lead you on the first steps of your Vision Quest.

1. What significant events to date would you consider to be your own rites of passage in your life? Why do you consider these rites of passage for you?

2. Take a moment to ask yourself what life event you are in the midst of? What dragons are you battling with right now? What life passage are you entering or emerging from? Rites of passage are thought to have three distinct phases. As you ponder over these questions, follow these phases of the Vision Quest.

    a. **Severance:** A separation from old ways of familiar lifestyle habits, perhaps even people.

    b. **Threshold:** The actual quest, a search for a vision or understanding of this transition, an inventory of inner resources and external surroundings to provide guidance through the transition period.

    c. **Incorporation:** A return from the quest to the community, with new insight and the ability to apply the knowledge from this experience as you progress in the development of your life.

3. During a Vision Quest, one receives the gift of a name to symbolize connectedness and groundedness. What name does the wind whisper in your ears?

7

6. GUIDED MENTAL IMAGERY

One relaxation technique for stress management is called guided mental imagery. In this technique, you think of a peaceful, calm image that promotes relaxation throughout your mind and body. To make it effective, you not only employ the imagination of your visual sense, but those of sound, smell, and touch as well. The combined creative effort of these sensations actually places you at the scene and promotes a deeper sense of relaxation. When people think of peaceful scenes, they usually think of a natural setting, somewhere where everyday problems are put in perspective with nature. It is no wonder that people take vacations in magnificent natural settings, like fabulous island beaches, majestic mountain peaks, or lone ocean dunes. The best scenes seem to be far away from the crowds and concerns of our everyday world, providing a retreat to nurture the soul.

Now it's time for you to use your creative thoughts and create some mental images of scenes that you feel are examples of perfect peaceful retreats. Describe five mental images or peaceful relaxing scenes that you would like to escape to momentarily. Use all your senses to place yourself at each scene. Be as elaborate with the description as you can so that each image can remain vivid in your memory.

7. DREAMS
The Language of Symbols

Dreams are a powerful language. They offer insight into the shadows of our unconscious mind. Carl Jung, world renowned psychologist and a pioneer in dream analysis, stated that dreams offer a basis of psychic balance, if only we would take the time to become more aware of them and reflect on their meaning. Although often expressed in a language of symbols, dreams may offer insight into ways to resolve our current problems. This insight begins with an awareness of dream fragments, followed by an interpretation process. As Jung suggested, the dream cannot be separated from the dreamer and, indeed, each of us is best suited to interpret our own dreams. A full interpretation, however, comes from looking at the dream image from every perspective to try to understand its meaning.

To enhance this dream awareness process, try leaving your journal by your bedstand and remind yourself before you fall asleep that you want to remember your dreams. Upon first waking, record whatever dream images or fragments you can recall. Then, mull over these images and listen to the thoughts they suggest. You may wish to revisit these dream images because their meaning is not always overtly obvious. Experts agree that not all dreams are significant, but the act of recording your images from the dream state may help you to deal more effectively with concerns and issues that you confront in your waking hours.

What dream do you recall from last night or a significant dream from any previous night? Do any objects that you recall seem to offer personal symbolism? After thinking about the fragments or sequences do they begin to make any sense to you?

8. CREATIVE PROBLEM SOLVING

"Imagination is more powerful than knowledge."
—Albert Einstein

The world has seven continents. Seven land masses. Seven environments. Although we each live on the same planet, we often have a special focus of our own world. As our world turns, we have different environments that ground our experiences, often many in the same day: the home environment, the work environment, the family environment, the play environment, and our natural environment, to name a few.

1. What do the continents of your world look like? How many continents or environments do you have? How large and where are they in relationship to each other with regard to importance in your life? Try making a sketch of the continents of your world, giving you a global view of your collective environments.

2. Just as international events capture our attention, sometimes causing us concern, frustration, or worry, so do our personal events or stressors that arise on the continents of our own world. Some continents, like Australia, may be very dormant or peaceful, while others, like Europe, are quite active. Take a moment to scan the continents of your life and make a list of the major headline stressors in each of your environments.

3. Many times when we are faced with a problem that stresses us, we tend to think of only one way to handle it. The ways we select are not always effective (e.g., avoidance, repression, hostility, or immobilization). But often, if not always, there are several ways to effectively deal with our problems. We just have to be creative. Creativity involves two phases: a *germination* phase, where imagination is employed to create an idea and a *harvest* phase, where a creative strategy is formulated to make the idea become a reality. In the germination phase, one explores for new ideas and then manipulates these ideas to one's environment. In the harvest phase, one judges the practicality of these ideas as viable options and then champions the cause with the most viable solution. Using your sense of creative thinking (both a germination and a harvest phase), think of two new viable options to successfully deal with one stressor in each environment.

9. A GIFT FROM THE SEA

Individuals are so very different, yet we all share so many common features, thoughts, even perceptions. Our makeup is so complex, yet similar from one person to another. We all have qualities about ourselves that we consider either strengths or weaknesses, and these certainly vary from person to person. Strengths can be magnified to bolster self-esteem. Weaknesses, too, can be magnified and become roadblocks to our human potential. The world is full of metaphors regarding the facets of our life. For example, a sea shell can be considered a metaphor, a symbol of ourselves.

After an extremely stressful event that changed the life of Anne Morrow Lindbergh and her husband, Charles, Anne took refuge on a secluded Hawaiian beach to find peace of mind and solace in her heart. In her book, *Gift from the Sea,* Lindbergh shares her personal thoughts as she cradled a series of sea shells in the palms of her hands, and reflected on the images they suggested, as well as the symbolism each offered.

The following thoughts and questions, inspired by Lindbergh's book, are provided to help you explore this metaphor. You don't need to have a sea shell in hand to do this exercise, but sometimes something tangible can really open up your thoughts.

1. Pick a shell from a collection of shells (if available) and hold it in your hand for a moment. Close your eyes and really feel it. What was it that attracted you to this particular shell? Take a moment to describe the shell you picked, its color, shape, texture, and size.

2. Many sea creatures have shells. Some have beautifully colored shells while some have incredible detail with ridges, points, and curls. Some shells are quite small, and others are very big. Some shells are very fragile while others seem the epitome of strength. Like sea creatures, we too have shells, though not quite as obvious. What is your shell like? Describe its shape, color, texture, and perhaps any other features that you wish to include, features that differentiate it from other shells.

3. Shells serve a purpose for sea creatures. They act as home as well as forms of protection; a base for security. The shells we have also act as a means of protection. Our shells, too, can offer a form of strength and security, but they can also overprotect. Does your own shell overprotect or is it a growing shell?

4. We all have strengths and weaknesses. Strengths are strong points of our personality or attributes that bring us favorable attention. Weaknesses, on the other hand, are what we perceive as our faults, insecurities, or attributes that we associate with negative connotations. List your strengths and, besides this list, write your weaknesses. Now take a careful look at this list. Sometimes strengths can actually be weaknesses while some weaknesses can be disguised as our strong points. For example, take a person who is well organized. This could be considered a weakness if it spills over into perfectionism. Sometimes, what we see as our weaknesses others see as our strengths and this may, in fact, be true. Many times it is the perceptions that make this difference. Now take a look at your list again. Are any of your strengths potential weaknesses and/or vice versa?

5. Feel free to add any comments, feelings, and even memories to this journal entry.

10. VALUES ASSESSMENT AND CLARIFICATION

Values. Those abstract ideals that shape our lives. Values are constructs of importance. They give the conscious mind structure. They can also give countries and governments structure. The Declaration of Independence is all about values, including "Life, liberty and the pursuit of happiness." Although values are intangible, often they are symbolized by material objects or possessions which can make values very real. What are some everyday examples of values? A partial list might include the following: love, peace, privacy, education, freedom, happiness, creativity, fame, integrity, faith, friendship, morals, health, justice, loyalty, honesty, and independence.

Where do values come from? We adopt values at a very early age, unconsciously, from people whom we admire, love, or desire acceptance from, like our parents, brothers and sisters, school teachers, clergy, etc. Values are often categorized into two groups: *basic* values, a collection of three to five instrumental values that are the cornerstones of the foundation of our personality, and *supporting* values, which augment our basic values. Through our development, we construct a value system, a collection of values that influences our attitudes and behaviors, all of which make up our personality.

As we mature our value system also changes as it becomes accountable for the way we think and behave. Like the earth's tectonic plates, our values shift in importance, causing our own earth to quake. These shifts are called *value conflicts* and they can cause a lot of stress. Classic examples of value conflicts include friendship vs. religious faith or social class (Romeo and Juliet), freedom vs. responsibility, and work vs. leisure (the American Dream). Conflicts in values can be helpful in our own maturing process if we work through the conflict to a full resolution. Problems arise when we tend to ignore the conflict and avoid clarifying our value system. The purpose of this journal theme is for you to take an honest look at your value system, assess its current status, and clarify unresolved issues associated with values in conflict. The following are some questions to help you in the process of values assessment and clarification.

1. Make a list of all the values you hold (values come from things that give you meaning and importance, yet are abstract in nature.

2. See if you can identify which of these values are *basic* or instrumental in your life at this point in your life and which *support* or augment your basic values.

3. How are your values represented in your life (i.e., a BMW may represent a symbol of wealth or freedom)?

4. Describe how your values influence your dominant thoughts, attitudes and beliefs.

5. Do you have any values that compete for priority with one another? If so, what are they and why is there a conflict?

6. What do you see as the best way to begin to resolve this conflict in values? Ask yourself if it is time to change the priority of your values or perhaps discard values that no longer give importance to your life.

11. ONE

A Holy Moment

Have you ever experienced a moment in your life where you became one with the universe? A special moment, a natural high, or a singular sensation that took your breath away and filled your heart with so much joy and wonder that you wanted to reach out, grab the world and hug it? More than likely, you have had a few singular sensations; several if you're lucky.

Psychologist Abraham Maslow called these *peak experiences*. Stress researcher Joan Borysenko refers to these as *holy moments,* and indeed they are very special. Like Maslow, Borysenko is of the opinion that not only do we need to be more receptive to these experiences, but that we also need to occasionally remind ourselves of these events to help lend emotional balance to the negative experiences we encounter throughout our lives. Search your memory bank. What holy moment comes to your mind at the thought of this suggestion? Perhaps it was seeing a deer jump into a thicket of woods while you were jogging on a dirt road, or while you were standing on a mountain top watching the sun reflect its crimson colors on a blanket of clouds near the horizon. Maybe it happened while making contact with a long lost friend or hugging your favorite dog or cat after a really bad day.

Close your eyes for a moment and think back to a very special moment when you felt a profound, if not divine, connection to the universe. A moment that transcended the everyday feelings and responsibilities we find ourselves routinely doing. Try to recall the emotional sensation that you experienced with this event. Then open your eyes and try to recapture the event on paper in as much detail as possible.

12. ANGER
The Fight Emotion

"He who angers you, conquers you."
—Elizabeth Kenny

Anger. The word itself brings to mind images of pounding fists, yelling, and smoke pouring out of one's ears and nose. But anger is as natural a human emotion as love. It is universal among all humans. Anger is a survival emotion; it's the fight component of the fight-or-flight response. We use anger to communicate our feelings, from impatience to rage. We employ anger to communicate boundaries and defend values. Studies show that the average person has between fourteen to fifteen anger episodes a day. These often arise when our expectations are not met upon demand. Although to feel angry is within the normal limits of human emotions, it is often mismanaged and misdirected. Unfortunately, we have been socialized to suppress our feelings of anger. As a result, anger either tears us apart from the inside (ulcers) or promotes intermittent eruptions of verbal or physical violence. In most, if not all, cases we do not deal with our anger correctly.

Research has shown that there are four very distinct ways in which people mismanage their anger. They include the following:

1. *Somatizers*: People who never show any signs of anger and internalize their feelings until eventually there is major bodily damage (i.e., ulcers, tempromandibular joint syndrome (TMJ), colitis, or migraines).

2. *Self-Punishers:* People who neither repress their anger nor explode, but rather deny themselves a proper outlet of anger due to guilty feelings (e.g., eating, exercise).

3. *Exploders*: Individuals who erupt like a volcano and spread their temper like hot lava destroying anyone and anything in its path with either verbal or physical abuse.

4. *Underhanders*: Individuals who sabotage or seek revenge to get even with someone through somewhat socially acceptable behavior (i.e., sarcasm, appearing late for meetings).

Although we tend to employ all of these styles at one time or another given the situation and prevailing circumstances, we tend to rely on one dominant style of mismanaged anger. What is your most dominant style? What situations provoke an anger response in you? How do you deal with these feelings of anger?

There are some ways to deal with anger correctly or perhaps even creatively. For example: (1) take a time-out from the situation, followed by a time-in to resolve the issue, (2) communicate your feelings diplomatically, (3) learn to outthink your anger, (4) plan several options to a situation, (5) lower personal expectations, and most importantly, (6) learn to forgive—make past anger pass. What are some ways you can vent your anger creatively?

Although anger is an emotion we all experience and should recognize when it arises, it is crucial to manage anger correctly. Sometimes just writing down on paper what gets you frustrated can be the beginning of the resolution process. And anger must be resolved.

13. FEAR
The Flight Emotion

"We have nothing to fear, but fear itself." Those immortal words spoken by F.D. Roosevelt during the Great Depression were expressed to calm an unsettled American public. Fear, like anger, is a very normal human emotion. We all experience it in our lives and more often than not, too many times in the course of our lives. Unlike anger, fear tends to be a difficult emotion to resolve. Feelings of anxiety or fear can trickle down from the mind to the body and wreak physical havoc from head to toe. While anger tends to make one want to defend turf and fight, fear makes one want to head for the hills and keep on running. The effects of fear can be exhausting. In fact, the effects do exhaust the body to the point of disease, illness, and sometimes death. Avoidance isn't the answer, but it's often the most employed technique used to deal with fear.

Although there are many situations that can promote anxiety, there are really only a handful of basic human fears that these situations fall under. They include the following:

1. **Fear of Failure:** A loss of self-worth through an event or action that promotes feelings of self-rejection.

2. **Fear of Rejection:** A loss of self-worth due to a perceived lack of acceptance from someone you attribute importance.

3. **Fear of the Unknown:** A fear based on a lack of inner faith to act without knowledge of future events or circumstances.

4. **Fear of Dying:** Pain, suffering, and uncertainty of death that produce anxiety.

5. **Fear of Isolation:** A fear of loneliness, uncomfortable feelings of self-solitude.

6. **Fear of Loss of Self-control:** The inability to determine factors that are and are not controllable, and a sense of not being able to control these circumstances in one's life.

Many of these basic human fears are very closely related and may overlap in some instances. Some fears may also dominate our way of thinking while others are unrelated to our lifestyles. Fear of any kind, however, is very much related to our level of self-esteem. At times, when we are down on ourselves, we are most susceptible to situations or circumstances that we perceive as fearful. Like anger, fears must be resolved. Resolution does not include ignoring or avoiding the problem. It is not easy and it takes work. When pursued properly, resolution is a continual process with many fruitful outcomes.

Sometimes by looking at our stressors, we can determine which fears they are associated with. The following questions may help you reflect on your current stressors that fall into this category.

1. Does one of these basic human fears tend to dominate your list of stressors? If so, why do you suppose that is the case?

2. How do you usually deal with your fears? Are you the type of person who hopes the circumstances surrounding these fears will go away?

3. What are some ways that will help you deal with some of these major fears?

14. MY PERSONAL TOTEM POLE

In the Pacific Northwest, native Americans established a longstanding tradition of storytelling by carving out on long wooden poles facial features of people and animals that represented a particular spirit or character of importance. The order in which they appeared on the pole unfolded into a special sequence of events which illustrated the highlights of a very important story. Some totem poles described tribal legends, stories of creation, mythology, and mystical happenings, while others related specific historical events of one's family heritage. The totem pole was a way to preserve the personal history.

   The totem pole idea is unique because the story told is based on particular people, animals, or spirits that brought influence or inspiration to a particular tribe, family, or individual. We each have our own historical story to tell that is also marked by certain events, objects, and people who have passed through and touched our lives. Personal totem poles might include special symbols that represent important events serving as personal landmarks, perhaps even as guides in the journey of our lives.

A maple leaf
A golden retriever
A sailboat
Cowboy boots
A passport
A wedding ring

   If you were to carve (describe) your life story on a long pole of wood by highlighting those symbols that represent the significant points that you remember in your life journey, what would they be? Take a few moments to sketch out your own personal totem pole that tells your personal history and then begin to recant this story, linking these symbolic images on paper so that one day you may pass it down through the generations of your own family.

15. MANDALA
OF THE HUMAN SPIRIT

A *mandala* is a circular-shaped object symbolizing unity with four separate quarters that represent directions of the universe, seasons of the years, or four points of reference. The origin of the mandala can be traced back to the dawn of humankind. Mandalas can vary in their size, design, colors, and symbolism. They are often used in the meditation practice as a focal point of concentration. In addition they are also used as decorations in many cultures from the Native American Medicine Wheel to art depictions of the Far East.

The mandala of the human spirit is a symbol of wholeness. It is a tool of self-awareness to allow you the opportunity to reflect on some of the components of the human spirit: a meaningful purpose in your life, personal values, and the implicit chance to learn more about yourself in the precious moments of solitude. Each quadrant represents a direction of your life with a symbol of orientation. The east is the initial point of origin. It represents the rising sun, the point of origin for each day. The focus of the mandala then moves southward, then to the west, and finally to the north.

Each focal point of the mandala of the human spirit provides questions for reflection. Take a few moments to reflect on the directions of the mandala to get a better perspective on the wellbeing of your human spirit. Then draw a circle dividing it into four areas and fill in the answers to the respective questions, creating a mandala of your very own human spirit.

NORTH

"The Wind – The Breath of Life."
What inspires you, guides, leads, or calls you?
What challenges you, what motivates you?
What are your stars, your shining lights?
What excites you and gives you energy?

WEST

"The setting sun"
"The promise of a new day."
"A future of possibilities."
What are your personal goals?
What are your hopes,
dreams, and fantasies?
What do you wish
to accomplish in your life?
What do you want to do
with your lifetime energy?

EAST

"The Orient"
(The East signifies
past experiences
& accomplishments.)
What are your proudest
achievements?
What lessons did you learn
from your achievements?
What values or beliefs did you
adopt through this process?
How do these contribute
to the meaning
of your life?

SOUTH

"The noon day sun"
"Sustenance in our lives"
What nurtures your personal growth?
What people give you a sense of community?
What brings pleasure and joy to your life?
What feeds your spirit?

17

16. INSPIRATION VS. INFLUENCE

Motivation is a complex phenomenon. It is thought to be comprised of two factors: those abstract qualities that inspire us from within, *intrinsic* (e.g., faith, hope, love, and willpower), and those external factors, often times more concrete in nature, *extrinsic* (e.g., money, rewards, trophies, people, and prizes), that influence our way of thinking, our emotions, and subsequent behaviors. Although we are open to both types of motivation, some individuals tend to be more intrinsically motivated or inspired. Others are greatly influenced by external factors. While both are natural characteristics of the human condition, generally, people who find inspiration from within have a sustained quality of inner peace. Conversely, individuals who tend to be easily influenced are often times less grounded and consequently more susceptible to stress.

Part of the motivation puzzle is the concept of goals: creating a game plan, a strategy to promote and nurture our levels of inspiration. Additionally, creating personal rewards for achieving our goals can help reinforce motivational attitudes. Sometimes just knowing what factors motivate you can be a helpful resource. These motivators can then be accessed when you are down in the dumps or in a rut, begging to be pulled out. Regarding personal influences, quite often we are not even aware of factors and people who influence us. One reason why we are more susceptible to the influence of others is because inspiration takes work. Sometimes it seems easier to float with the tide than to swim.

Are you more intrinsically inspired or extrinsically motivated? What typically gets you out of bed and cruising down life's highway? What parts of life do you find to be inspiring? Are you the kind of person who makes goals and then rewards yourself for the accomplishments of these goals? What things, events, or happenings do you find really drain your energy level and/or self-esteem? What are some ways to boost your level of motivation and give yourself a jump start?

17. STRESS BAROMETER CHECK

Weather reports, economic forecasts, news sound-bites, and mail are all bits of information we assemble to gain a clearer understanding of our collective environments. Heart rate, blood pressure, ventilation, and muscle tension are clinical vital signs used to determine an initial health status report. Monitored regularly, they too can help us understand how our bodies absorb the events of our lives.

Sight, sound, taste, smell, and feel are sensations that help the mind gather and process information that our environments send us. And too much information can overload the circuits. Figuratively speaking, this can blow a fuse. The result is stress-related disease and illness, from the common cold, to coronary heart disease, and perhaps even cancer. Research now suggests that 70%–80% of all disease and illness is associated with stress. Therefore, it is a very good idea to monitor your stress levels periodically, as well as the potential repercussions they might have on your body.

Take a moment to contemplate your mind-body relationship. Scope yourself top to bottom, head to toe, and check for any signs or symptoms that could be a result of too much wear and tear on the body from perceived stress. Are there any "hot spots," some part of your body that is the target of your perceived stress? Next, check your current level of sensory input (deprivation vs. overload). Both can cause stress. If either seems to be evident, what can you do to remedy this situation? Take a pen in hand and jot down what you find with your stress barometer check.

Mental imagery can be a powerful tool to heal the body. From the research of O. Carl Simonton, coauthor of the best seller, *Getting Well Again,* and Dr. Bernie Siegel, author of *Love, Medicine & Miracles*, we have learned that some cancer patients actually have had their tumors go into remission by thinking of metaphorical images to heal the body. Additional studies have shown that imagery can be used to assist in the healing processes of such health problems, including hypertension (unclogged highways), ulcers (darning socks), tension headaches (ironing wrinkled clothes), you name it. All it takes is a little creativity—generating an idea and implementing the idea into reality. If you happen to have a hot spot or a manifestation of stress in your body, can you think of a metaphorical image to initiate the healing process? Give it a try. You may even want to map out this hot spot on an image of your body and write out a mental image to heal it.

18. DREAMS REVISITED

We all have dreams, although remembering them is not always easy. But there are occasions when a certain dream seems to be replayed in our mind over the course of months, perhaps even years. *Recurring dreams*, as they are commonly called, may only have a short run on the mind's silver screen or they may last throughout the course of our life time. These dreams, perhaps foggy in detail, surface occasionally in the conscious state and the story they tell is all too familiar.

It is commonly believed that recurring dreams symbolize a hidden insecurity or a stressful event that has yet to be resolved. They don't have resolved endings. While there is much to the dream state that is still unknown, it is believed that dreams are images that the unconscious mind creates to communicate to the conscious mind in a language all its own. This form of communication is not a one-way street. Messages can be sent to the unconscious mind in a normal waking state as well.

Through the use of mental imagery, you can script the final scenes of a recurring dream with a happy ending. What seems to be the final scene of a dream is actually the beginning of the resolution process. The following is a true story: Once there was a young boy who had an afternoon paper route. One day while delivering papers, a large black German shepherd jumped out of the bushes and attacked the boy. The owner called the dog back, but not before the dog drew blood. As the boy grew into adulthood his love for dogs never diminished, but several times a year he awoke in a sweat from a recurring dream he had had once too often. **The Dream:** "It was dark and I was walking through the woods at night. Out from behind one of the trees came this huge black dog. All I could see were his teeth and hear his bark. I tried to yell for help but nothing came out of my throat. Just as he lunges for me, I awake in a panic."

With a little thought and imagination, some work was placed on drafting a final scene to bring closure to this dream story. **Final Scene:** "I am walking through the woods at night with a flashlight, a bone, and a can of mace. This time when the dog lunges at me, I shine the light in his eyes and spray mace in his face. He whines and whines and then I tell him to sit. He obeys. I put the bone by his nose and he looks at me inquisitively. Then he licks the bone and starts to bite into it. I begin to walk away and the dog gets up to follow, bone in mouth. I stop and look back and he stops. He wags his tail. The sky grows light as the sun begins to rise, and the black night fades into pink and orange clouds. As I walk back to my house, I see the dog take his new find down the street. I open the door and walk upstairs and crawl back into bed." It has been five years, and this individual has never had this dream again.

Ultimately we are the creators of our dreams. We are the writers, directors, producers, and actors of our dreams. Although drafting a final scene is no guarantee that the issues that produce recurring dreams are resolved, it is a great starting point toward the resolution process, a time for reflection that may open up the channels of communication between the conscious and unconscious mind. Is there a recurring dream that you have that needs a final scene to be complete? Write out your recurring dream and give it a final scene.

19. ART THERAPY

Many of our thoughts and emotions are hard to express in words. Not always, but often a visual picture rich in color, texture, and style can best describe how we feel. Art therapy is used in many settings (hospitals, prisons, stress management classes, corporate executive wellness programs) to help individuals learn to express themselves and their thoughts and feelings, visually in a way that words cannot adequately describe. Many times drawings can communicate thoughts from the unconscious that the conscious mind can begin to decipher and understand for a more honest picture of the real you. For example, colors used and the proportion of objects or people can connote specific moods or personal meaning. Exploring thoughts, memories, and feelings from the right side of the brain can often lead to a clearer understanding of where these come from and perhaps what they represent. Illustrations, when combined with a narrative, can also be used to enhance memories of journal entries from vacations or special events.

What does it take to try this? Some desire and a little bit of imagination. You don't have to be an artist. You only need crayons, colored pencils, paint or pastels, some paper, and a desire to illustrate what's on your mind to paper. As children we love to draw, but as people get older we shy away from drawing because of embarrassment. Like other journal assignments, this too is confidential. No one is going to look at it, no one is going to analyze or judge it, nor should you when you complete the picture you have started. For this reason, there is no need to feel inhibited. Whether your skills produce stick figures or create at the level of Rembrandt or Renoir, give it a try.

The following suggestions are ideas used in art therapy classes. They are only suggestions. Feel free to augment these in any way that you feel most comfortable.

1. With your eyes closed, draw a line on a page and then open your eyes and from what you see, finish the picture to make whatever you would like.

2. Illustrate something that describes your best attributes or what best describes who you are or draw yourself.

3. Identify one area of your body that you feel is a target organ, a recipient of your stress. From this, use your imagination to think up a mental image to cure or restore homeostasis to this part of your body and then draw this image on paper.

4. Draw a mandala. Your mandala. A mandala is like a personal coat of arms. In this case, a coat of arms of wholeness. Start with a circular shape and from this divide it into four equal (or unequal) areas. Add to this items or colors, or include anything that you feel gives you inspiration and wholeness (to be healthy means to be whole).

5. Draw a representation of your feelings of either anger or fear.

6. Draw whatever you like, whatever comes to mind, for whatever reason.

21

20. CONFRONTATION
OF A STRESSOR

It happens to us all the time. Someone or something gets us frustrated, and we literally head for the hills, either avoiding it altogether or ignoring the situation by hoping it will go away. But situations like this that we ignore typically come back to haunt us. In the short run, avoidance looks appealing, even safe. But in the long run, it is bad policy. Really bad policy. We avoid confrontation because we want to avoid the emotional pain associated with it. The pain our ego suffers. Handled creatively, diplomatically, and rationally, the pain is minimal, and it often leads to a positive growth experience of our human spirit. After all, this is what life is all about; to achieve our full human potential.

The art of peaceful confrontation involves a strategy of creativity, diplomacy, and grace to ensure that you come out the victor, not the victim. In this sense, confrontation doesn't mean a physical battle, rather a mental, emotional, or spiritual battle. Unlike a physical battle where knights wear armor, this confrontation requires that you let down the walls of your ego long enough to resolve the fear or anger associated with the stressor. The weapons of this confrontation are self-assertiveness, self-reliance, and faith. There is no malice, spite, or deceit involved. Coping mechanisms that aid the confrontation process include, but are not limited to, the following strategies: communication, information seeking, cognitive reappraisal, social engineering, and values assessment and clarification.

We all encounter stressors that we tend to run away from. Now it is time to gather your internal fortitude and make a personal plan to successfully confront your stressor. When you initiate this confrontation plan, you come out the victor with a positive resolution and a positive feeling of accomplishment. First, reexamine your list of top ten stressors. Then, select a major stressor to confront and resolve. Prepare a plan of action, and then carry it out. When you return, write about it; what the stressor was, what your strategy was, how it worked, how you feel about the outcome, and perhaps most importantly, what you learned from this experience.

21. MY POSITIVE ATTRIBUTES

Someone once calculated that the mineral contents and physiological properties of the human body have a net worth of approximately $2.65. Many estimates, however, have been calculated to appraise the real value of a human life with one unanimous decision: every human being is priceless. No monetary value can adequately replace us. No amount of money can compensate for the capabilities of the mind, body, and spirit. This fact alone would make you think that each individual has a lot going in his or her direction. In fact, we all do, it is just that more often than not it never seems that way. We tend to dwell on our negative characteristics and this focus can really impede our quality of life. Perhaps the roots of American negativism can be traced to the dogma of Puritanism, where personal worth was believed to be equal to the work you did, and no amount of work was ever enough. It's a fact, however, that Americans typically tend to take a very negative attitude toward themselves. Compound this with the concept of the self-fulfilling prophecy and you have a no-win situation regarding self-esteem and successful strategies for stress management.

We all have many positive attributes, those qualities that we take pride in, from our physical, mental, emotional and spiritual makeup. We need to be reminded of these qualities to boost our self-esteem when the gray clouds of life start to collect over our heads. Take a moment to reflect on your positive attributes: those qualities that make you unique. Select from all areas of your total wellbeing, including your physical, intellectual, emotional, and spiritual dimensions. Write them in a list, perhaps even describing each one and why you consider it to be an asset. If you can't come up with at least ten, ask a few friends to suggest what they see as your positive attributes. You may be surprised to find what they see in you that you may fail to recognize in yourself. On days when you need a boost in your self-esteem, refer to this list.

23

22. UNWRITTEN LETTERS
A Resolution Process

Many is the time we wish to communicate with someone we love, like, or just know well. For one reason or another, whether it be anger, procrastination or not finding the right words at the right time, we part ways. As a result, those special feelings never seem to be fully resolved. There was once a college coed whose former boyfriend took his life. In the note left behind, he specifically mentioned this student and the words seemed to haunt her for what seemed like an eternity. Through some counseling, she decided to write him a letter to express her feelings of anger, sorrow, loneliness, and love. Through her words, her letter began the resolution process and ultimately her path toward inner peace.

This theme of resolution through letter writing has been the subject of a great many books, plays, and movies. In one movie made for television entitled *Message to my Daughter*, a young mother with a newborn baby discovers she has terminal cancer. As a part of her resolution process, she recorded several cassette tapes with personal messages to her daughter. Many father-son relationships also fall into this category, where emotional distance becomes an impassable abyss. It is a common theme.

It has been said that, with the recent advances in technology, from the cellular telephone to the microchip, Americans are writing fewer and fewer personal letters. Sociologists worry that future generations will look back at this time period, the information high-tech age, and never really know what individuals were actually feeling and thinking because there will be few, if any, written entries to trace these perceptions. Moreover, psychologists agree that many of today's patients are troubled and unable to articulate their thoughts and feelings completely, thereby resulting in unresolved stress.

This journal entry revolves around the theme of resolution. The following are some suggestions that might inspire you to draft a letter to someone you have been meaning to write. Now is your chance.

1. Compose a letter to someone you were close to who has passed away, or perhaps someone who you have lost contact with for a long period of time. Tell that person what you have been up to, perhaps any major changes in your life, or changes that you foresee occurring in the months or years ahead. If there are any unresolved feelings associated with this person, try expressing your thoughts and feelings in the appropriately crafted words so that you can resolve these feelings and come to a sense of lasting peace.

2. Write a letter to yourself. Imagine that you have one month to live. What would you do in these last thirty days? Assume that there are no limitations. Whom would you see? Where would you visit? What would you do? Why?

3. Pretend that you now have a baby son or daughter. What would you like to share with your child now, should, for some reason, you not have the opportunity to do so later in life. What would you like your child to know about you? For example, perhaps you would share things that you wanted to know about your parents or grandparents, which now are pieces missing in your life.

4. Write a letter to anyone you wish for whatever reason.

23. A LOG CABIN EXPERIENCE
Creative Writing

For many people, a log cabin tucked away in the mountains exudes romance and freedom; a communal spell with nature, a chance to leave life's drudgeries behind, a time to nurture the soul and rejuvenate the human spirit, and even clean out the cobwebs of the mind. At the turn of the nineteenth century, many mountain cabins were built for such escapes. Often the cabins contained a log book, where visitors could share a word or two, such as a memorable experience or even a story for future cabin guests, as well as be entertained with the exploits and stories of previous cabin visitors.

The chance for solitude high in the mountains often stimulates creative expression. Creative writing can be a healthy expression of thoughts, ideas, and feelings through the eyes of another character, in the third person voice or the first person in a new time period. Close your eyes for a moment and imagine you are sitting by the stone hearth of a large glowing fire under the huge rack of deer antlers. Smell the pitch of the pine as it sparks and crackles in the fire. See the shadows of the fire dance on the log cabin walls, and feel the warmth of the lambskin rug underneath as you sip a cup of hot tea or coffee. Imagine now, that it is your turn to draft an entry into the cabin's visitors log. What creative story do you have to pass along in these pages?

MIRABELLE AT BEAVER CREEK

24. THE THINGS I TAKE FOR GRANTED

Almost instinctively, humans have given thanks since they first set foot on earth. From animal sacrifices to banquet feasts to silent moments of praise, the occasion to show appreciation for the smallest of gifts to some of life's greatest pleasures is very much a part of the human condition. A unique tradition was established on the shores of the New World several hundred years ago when English immigrants and native Americans sat down to perhaps the most famous autumn feast ever created, Thanksgiving, and appropriately thereafter it became a yearly event.

It is easy to give thanks and praise in times of joy and happiness. It is rarely thought of, however, in times of crisis. Actually, stress can produce some very ungrateful attitudes. Stressful events tend to cloud the mind with thoughts of frustration and anguish, some directed inward, most directed outward, and these can leave little room for much else. When the Pilgrims sat down to the first turkey dinner, times were hard. There was no indoor plumbing, no drug stores, no credit cards, and no daycare centers. Life was a real challenge. But in that challenge, life was reduced to the simplest of terms. The challenge was survival. In our day and age, survival is pretty much a given fact. The question isn't "Will I survive?," but rather "How well can I live?" Although theoretically, the high-tech age has improved the quality of life, it also seems to drag with it the pressures that seem to negate this standard of quality.

More stress and less time to enjoy life's simple pleasures can often make it difficult to give adequate time to sit back every now and then and appreciate the little things that make life special. Stress can act as blinders to our field of vision. By consciously taking these blinders off, we can see the whole picture in better focus. Taking things for granted is as much a part of human nature as giving thanks. But so often we don't know what we've got "til it's gone." A list of things that you take for granted could be endless. But if you were to stop and think for a moment on what some of these might include, just what would they be and why?

25. WORDS FROM A SONG
Reflections on Personal Relationships

Have you ever heard a song, and after listening to the lyrics, thought to yourself, I know somebody who really needs to hear these words. In fact, you may actually feel like buying the album or compact disc and mailing it to that "someone" with an anonymous note saying "Drop what you're doing right now, sit and listen to the words of this song and reflect on its meaning."

We have all felt like this at some point in our lives. Sometimes, it seems like poets and song writers corner the market on the expression of thoughts and feelings. Given the chance, we might do as good a job ourselves. But there appears to be a mental passage in which words travel more accessibly when a melody accompanies them. The message really can hit home at the soul. Here are the facts: relationships are tough to initiate, hard work to maintain, and, let's face it, there's no graceful way in which they end. Through it all, communication is essential and sometimes words we hear in a song really convey the message.

Let us turn the tables for a moment. Pretend that someone you know sent you the words to a song and asked you to reflect on the song's meaning as it relates to you and the respective relationship. The following songs were selected to represent a variety of relationships: girlfriend, boyfriend, parental, and inner-self relationships. If you know these songs and have the lyrics at hand, select one and read the words and ponder the message they communicate. Reflect on these for a while and then write down your thoughts as they come to mind. Should you happen to have a favorite song lyric which might better serve this purpose, please feel free to write it down and then reflect on it.

Selected Songs

"The Stranger," Billy Joel (*self-relationship*).
"Hasten Down the Wind," Warren Zevon (*girlfriend relationships*).
"Thinking of Leaving," Cheryl Wheeler (*divorce, parental relationships*).
"The Greatest Love of All," M. Masser & L. Creed (*self-relationship*).
"You Don't Know Me," Eddie Arnold (*boyfriend/girlfriend relationships*).
"If He's Ever Near," Karla Bonoff (*boyfriend relationships*).
"Father and Son," Cat Stevens (*parental relationships*).

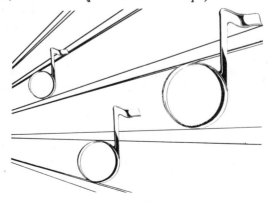

26. ROLE MODELS AND HEROES

"Everything I do and say with anyone makes a difference."
—Gita Bellen

It has been said that since the advent of television and video technology, the culture of American heroes has changed significantly, if not disappeared altogether. In the late 1980's a popular weekly magazine conducted a survey identifying current American heroes. It was learned that the top twenty-five people selected were either Hollywood television actors or rock star musicians. People, it now seems, are very fascinated with the ideals of fame and fortune.

In days gone by there was a different fascination that created legends, catapulted individuals to hero status, and inspired people to follow in their footsteps. The qualities of early American heroes and role models were the inventors, the explorers, the philosophers, and the movers and shakers of the world. They were people like Ben Franklin, Florence Nightingale, Babe Ruth, Booker T. Washington, Mark Twain, Lewis and Clark, Amelia Earhart, Carl Jung, Abraham Lincoln, Eleanor Roosevelt, Charles Lindberg, Thomas Edison, Harriet Tubman, Thoreau, Rosa Parks, and John Glenn, to name a few.

It's quite well known that we all are capable of heroic deeds and there are a great many unrecognized heroes currently in our midsts. These are just ordinary people who do extraordinary things. People who give 100% effort against insurmountable odds and come out on top. If you were to ask a child who his or her hero is, you might likely hear the reply "Mom" or "Dad." In the course of a lifetime, however, a great many people influence us, some we never meet, but perhaps only hear or read about.

When you stop to think about it, some people can have a profound positive influence on our lives. Perhaps more than we recognize. The following questions are provided as food for thought regarding your role models and life heroes.

1. What person would you say has had the greatest influence on your life? Why?

2. Most people model their adult behavior and even thoughts/perceptions as a result of a synthesis of several people and the influence they have had. What people do you admire and tend to model some of your thoughts and behaviors?

3. If you could have lunch with anyone, currently living in this time period or perhaps another time altogether, someone who you have never had lunch with before and you will never have lunch with again, who would you like to break bread with and tap into for an hour, and why?

4. We not only have role models and heroes, but we are role models. We not only absorb the light, but we also reflect it too. Who in your life have you been a role model to? Whom have you touched, inspired, and reflected light toward?

27. ONE PERSONAL WISH!

Aladdin had three and Pinocchio had one with a rebate. Perhaps not a single day goes by that we don't wish for something. From birthday cake candles to Thanksgiving dinner wishbones, the wish is as much a part of American culture as apple pie and baseball. In the Orient wise men are occasionally heard saying to young children the Chinese curse, "May all your wishes come true." Likewise, Oscar Wilde once said, "When the Gods want to punish you, they answer your prayers." When wishes are based on greed, trouble undoubtedly lies ahead. But often, wishes can be the seeds of creativity, and creativity can have a host of wonderful events and possibilities.

Wishes consist of one part hope, one part love, and one part sweat. Although the fulfillment of our wishes, prayers and dreams may take longer than we would like, wishes can come true. Fairy tales aside, if you were to be granted one personal wish, what would it be and, perhaps most importantly, why?

28. CONTROL
A Double-Edged Sword

"God, grant me the serenity to accept the things I cannot change, the courage to change the things I can and the wisdom to know the difference." The "Serenity Prayer," by Reinhold Neibuhr embodies one of the cornerstone principles of the recovery program initiated through Alcoholics Anonymous.

The unyielding message of the serenity prayer is about control. Control is a paradox. It can be perceived as either good or bad. For this reason, it can be compared to a double-edged sword. To master this tool and not inflict self-damage, one must understand and recognize what one does and does not have control over, and the wisdom to know the difference. Many people use control as manipulative behavior. Often they try to control others and events because they find these easier to control than their own thoughts and actions. People who employ manipulative behavior mistake control for responsibility. This manipulative behavior can become addictive. Each episode of control is like the next "fix" — a false inflation of one's self-worth until the next controllable opportunity. The result can be a vicious cycle, and it can be a very unhealthy behavior. Conversely, control is also said to be one of three prime characteristics (in conjunction with challenge and commitment) in what psychologists now refer to as the *hardy personality* or *stress-resistant personality*. Unlike manipulative behavior, this perspective focuses on self-control as a function of willpower.

Are you a master swordsman with a strong sense of self-control, or does the action of manipulative behavior metaphorically cut and nick your hands? Do people and events that you seem to have no control over frustrate you? Do you spend a lot of energy against the flow, managing events that you feel only you can do well. Do you or have you mistaken responsibility for control? How is your sense of willpower? And finally, what are some ways you can become a master swordsman with the power of self-control?

29. THE CHILD WITHIN

To see a universe of life in a few blades of grass while lying face down on a lawn under the summer sun. To catch yourself laughing at the silliest idea or crying with remorse without any inhibition to stop. To believe in the power of magic and be suspended in time with curiosity. To see life as an adventure and be swept away in the colors of a rainbow to a far away land. To love without conditions. These are the precious moments of childhood. Conversely, childhood can be filled with many dark and lonely moments as well; battles of sibling rivalry, abusive parents, ridicule from our peers, and unending hours of loneliness. At times, childhood can be filled with both glorious naiveté and painful abandonment. Some of these aspects of our youth fade too quickly as the seasons of our life spin faster and faster toward adulthood, while others linger on with many unresolved feelings.

Despite the maturation process into our adult years, within each and every one of us there still remains a child; a child who continually needs to be nurtured, loved, and protected. Let's pretend for a moment that you could actually meet a younger version of yourself at about age four to five. Behind the ruffled hair, freckles, wide eyes, and missing tooth is a child longing to be loved and begging for acceptance. With years, even decades of experience behind you now, what would you say to this child? What could you say to comfort, love or nurture this child within you. Ponder for a moment on some comforting words of advice, some thoughts of love that you might have liked to have heard at that age to help you in the transition into your adolescence and adulthood.

Also, as with any good conversation, there is dialogue from each side. Listen closely to the child within and discuss what he or she is begging to tell you. Perhaps your inner child will suggest that it has been too long since you lay face down on a summer lawn under the sun and explored blades of grass. Perhaps he or she will tell you that it's okay to cry or laugh out loud again or to explore your sense of creativity and curiosity. We have much to learn from the child within us. Share the thoughts of this conversation with your younger self.

30. THE GARDEN OF EDEN

Sigmund Freud is credited with saying that the average adult thinks about sex every thirty seconds. While the time interval may vary from person to person, there's no doubt that our sexual drive, along with our drive for nourishment and sleep, is an important part of our daily makeup. Consequently, sexual drive can contribute to much frustration and stress. Regardless of gender, individuals become sexually active during puberty around the ages of eleven to thirteen. It is not until a person reaches adulthood at the age of eighteen that one's sexual behavior is fully recognized and accepted. Between puberty and adulthood there exists a five-to nine-year period of potential personal frustration.

Social, cultural, and religious mores and expectations only confound this issue with rules, laws, and dogma linking the approval of sexual activity with marriage. What can be really confusing are all the mixed messages from the media and advertising industry that are loaded with sexual overtones and innuendoes. Moreover, there are many issues and concerns adding to this frustration including unplanned pregnancy, sexually transmitted diseases, rejection, birth control and contraception, value conflicts, date rape, homosexuality, and guilt. Later in the life cycle, more issues arise that are related to sex anxiety including not being able to conceive, low sperm count, sexual addiction, impotency, sexual inactivity, and sexual dissatisfaction. This list goes on and on.

Unlike our other drives, human sexuality carries the heavy burden of incredible responsibility. As a result, the implications surrounding sexuality can be very stressful. Without a doubt, good communication is a crucial factor in reducing some of the anxiety regarding human sexuality, but much of the communication must initiate with ourselves, to ourselves, and from there to those we are intimately involved with. Now is a good time to initiate this communication with yourself. Is sexuality a current stressor in your life? Take a moment to do some soul searching on this issue.

31. SPIRITUAL WELLBEING

Human spiriuality is so complex that it seems to defy an adequate definition and description. It is often compared to love, self-esteem, faith, and so many human characteristics that seem to be related to it. This we do know. Human spirituality involves a strong personal self-relationship as well as connectedness or strong relationships with others, a strong personal value system, and a meaningful purpose in life. Unlike religions that have integrated these components, human spirituality has no rules, no dogma, and no set agenda. These concepts are related, but separate entities. Psychiatrist Carl Jung once said, "Every crisis over the age of thirty is spiritual in nature." There is a definite relationship between stress and spirituality.

Over the years, M. Scott Peck, author of *The Road Less Traveled,* has studied the concepts of human spirituality, and he has developed a four-stage model to understand spiritual development. Each stage has many layers; and indeed, some people seem to hover somewhere between stages. Be that as it may, these categories can help us to focus on our spiritual path.

1. *Chaotic Antisocial Individual:* A person who is manipulative, unprincipled, and governed by selfish pleasure under spiritual bankruptcy. His or her lifestyle is unorganized, in chaos or crisis, and headed for the rocks, which in turn causes much pain. All blame is externalized and projected on others.

2. *Formal Institutionalized Individual:* In this stage a sudden conversion occurs where a person finds shelter in an institution (prison, military, or church) for security, structure, rules, and guidance. People in this stage see God as a loving but punitive figure, an "Irish cop in the sky." God is personified with human characteristics (i.e., a human face, a masculine pronoun, He, His, etc.). Institutions do, however, make some order out of the chaos.

3. *Skeptic Individual:* A person who, in searching for answers, rejects the institution that claims to have the answers. This person is a "Born-again Atheist," a person who doesn't buy into the system of rules and dogma any more, but still believes that there is something out there and wants to find it. According to Peck, this is a crucial stage of development.

4. *Mystic Communal Individual:* An individual who is actively searching for new answers to life's age-old questions, but who feels comfortable knowing that he or she may never find the answers. This person's vision of God is as internal as it is external. Additionally, such an individual sees the need for community or bonding and tries to foster this. Finally, individuals who reach this stage realize that upon arrival, it is only the beginning.

Most importantly, spiritual wellbeing is an unfolding, an evolution of higher consciousness. Spirituality is also very personal, and we each travel on our path at our own pace.

1. How would you define spirituality?

2. What state of wellbeing is your human spirit currently in?

3. What stage of development in Peck's model do you see yourself in?

4. Is your perception of God personified?

5. Do you have a relationship with God? If so, how strong or weak is it? What steps could you take to improve this relationship?

32. POSITIVE AFFIRMATION STATEMENTS

Positive affirmation statements are thoughts or expressions that you repeat to yourself to boost your self-esteem. These words of inspiration highlight the positive aspects of your own personality traits and characteristics that enhance and nurture your self-esteem. They are expressions that build confidence, provide inspiration, lift the spirit to rise above mediocrity and function at your highest human potential.

It is easy to give yourself negative feedback about almost anything. We each have a critic who, metaphorically, sits on our shoulder and whispers negative thoughts in our ear. The media does this too, striking at our insecurities through subliminal and overt advertising with over 1,500 messages per day. In addition, we often interpret feedback to be negative from family, friends, and people who pass in and out of our lives. But worst of all, perhaps as a learned behavior, we continually feed ourselves negative thoughts, which continually deflate self-esteem.

The use of positive affirmation statements is really a behavior modification technique used in conjunction with relaxation techniques (deep breathing or mental imagery) to train the mind to give the battered ego positive strokes, and strengthen self-esteem. Although there are no specific rules, there are some guidelines that can make these positive affirmations work for you. 1. Phrase your affirmation in the present tense such as "I am a lovable person." 2. Phrase your affirmation in the most positive way. 3. Make your affirmation simple, clear, and precise. 4. Choose an affirmation that feels right for you.

The following is a sample of some positive affirmation statements that others have used for this purpose. A positive affirmation statement should be a personal thought or expression. If, however, at first you cannot think of one, feel free to use one or more of these. Eventually, you may want to take a moment to think up one that is personal to you. Positive affirmation statements should be somewhat short; something you can repeat to yourself in one breath.

1. Damn, I'm good.
2. I am one with the Tao.
3. Love is the answer.
4. I am calm and relaxed.
5. I have confidence in myself.
6. I am an important piece of the whole.
7. I am a lovable person.
8. I radiate success!
9. I am worthy of being loved.
10. Your positive affirmation statement _____.

Now that you have chosen your positive affirmation statement, write down five places or times of day that you can say this to yourself to reinforce this message. Then, do it!

33. EMBRACE THE SHADOW

Have you ever noticed how often we judge other people and make note of their imperfections, especially when we feel violated or victimized by their actions? How often do you find fault with others who cross your path, or worse, become obstacles on it? And have your ever noticed how much easier it is to find fault with someone when you have a reason not to like him or her? Have you noticed that it is the easiest time to pass judgment when you're most stressed? If you feel this way, you are not alone. And if you are like most people, you may find yourself pointing your finger at several people in the course of a day who *seem* to make your life miserable.

It has often been said that those flaws and foibles that we point out in others are merely reflections of our own imperfections. As a defense to protect our ego, we pass them off on others because it is painful to acknowledge them in our own being. Psychologist Carl Jung called this the *shadow*, the dark side of human nature that resides within each of us. It was Jung's belief that those who refuse to acknowledge their own shortcomings, their dark side, yet project this on others, will constantly do battle with stress. Jung was of the opinion that we must not only acknowledge our dark side, but come to terms with it, embrace it, if you will. For until it is acknowledged and "domesticated," we will never truly be at peace with ourselves.

So how do we learn to "embrace the shadow?" First, perhaps it is important to recognize that each human being has a shadow. Now, having done this, call to mind one or two people whom you feel at odds with, pinpoint what it is in these people that you dislike, despise, or distrust, and then write these characteristics down and explain why. Next, run a personal inventory on your own thoughts and actions, the dark side of your personality, and see if there is some commonality with the individual(s) you just listed. Remember, where there is light, there will always be a shadow, and having a dark side doesn't make you a bad person. Describe some ways that you can learn to embrace your shadow.

34. HUMOR IS THE BEST MEDICINE
Things That Make Me Smile and Laugh

Life is full of absurdities, incongruities, and events that tickle our funny bone. For instance, Charlie Chaplin once got third place in a Charlie Chaplin look-alike contest. Since the day Norman Cousins checked out of a hospital room in 1964, into a hotel room across the street, and literally laughed his way back to health from a life-threatening disease, the medical world has stood up and taken notice. Humor really is good medicine.

Today, there is a whole new scientific discipline called *psychoneuroimmunology* (PNI), the study of the relationship between the mind and the body and the effects each has on the other. It is no secret that negative emotions (e.g., anger, fear, guilt, worry, depression, loneliness, etc.) can have a detrimental effect on the body, manifesting into disease and illness. Although there is much to be understood, we now know that, just as negative emotions can have a negative effect on the body, positive emotions (e.g., joy, love, hope, and the feelings associated with humor) can have a positive effect on the body by speeding the healing process and promoting total wellbeing.

Humor is a great stress reducer. Humor acts as a coping mechanism to help us deal with life's hardships. It softens the walls of the ego, makes us feel less defensive, unmasks the naked truth in a comical way, and often gives us a clearer perspective and focus in our everyday lives. Comic relief is used in many stress management programs, hospitals, and work settings to reduce the effects of stress. Stress is often associated with negative attitudes that really deflate self-esteem. A preponderance of negative emotions can taint our view of the world around us, perpetuating the stress cycle. There has to be a balance! What researchers are now discovering is that we need to incorporate these positive emotions to achieve this balance, and humor is one of the answers.

Although one could turn to the television to catch a few laughs, the greater variety of humor vehicles (books, movies, live comedians, and music) one is exposed to, the more rewarding the riches. Sometimes all we have to do is dig through our memory to find a tickler.

1. How would you rate your sense of humor? Do you exercise it often? Do you exercise it correctly? Offensive humor (sarcasm, racial, and sexist humor, and practical jokes) can actually promote stress. What are some ways to augment your sense of humor?

2. What is your favorite kind of humor? Parody, Slapstick, Satire, Black Humor, Nonsense, Irony, Puns? What type of humor do you fall back on to reduce your stress?

3. What would you consider to be the funniest moment(s) of your life?

4. What are some of the funniest moments that you can recall from any situation that the mere thought of puts a grin or secret smile on your face?

5. In the song, "My Favorite Things," Julie Andrews sang about a host of things that flooded her mind with joy and brought a smile to her face. What would your list include?

6. Make a list of things to do, places to go, and people to see to lift your spirits when the occasion calls for it.

35. A TRAUMATIC EXPERIENCE

Into our lives a little rain must fall, but it seems that once or twice we encounter a devastating flood and, subsequently, get pulled under and washed away in the currents. Broken bones, the death of a close friend or loved one, and child abuse are just a handful of life's many tragedies. "Tragedy," it is said, "keeps a person humble." But is can also leave several scars, including physical, mental, emotional, and spiritual, that may take a lifetime to heal.

Reactions may vary, but immediately after experiencing a tragedy, people talk nervously. This is one of the initial manifestations of grief. This stage is often followed by withdrawal and, eventually, a slow reemergence into society. These types of experiences from years ago, can also affect our outlook and behaviors on several issues, often unknowingly. If you have been spared a personal tragedy, consider yourself lucky. If you have experienced an event of this nature and wish to recount it here, feel free to do so. Peace.

36. TIME AND MONEY

It has been said that two of the biggest constraints to leisure are time and money, or the lack thereof. It is no coincidence that these two factors are also two of the leading causes of stress. It is highly unlikely that a check for a million dollars waiting for you in the mailbox tomorrow would solve your lifelong financial concerns. Neither would an extra hour in the day nor an extra day in the week give you more time to get your work done. We are creatures of habit and chances are that if we had more time and money, it would be spent much the same way as done previously.

While we may not receive a million dollars or have extra hours in the day, we do have several resources to help us budget these constraints. In the information age of high technology, we are bombarded with interruptions. Time management isn't a luxury, it is a necessity. The keys to good time management include learning how to prioritize responsibilities, learning to organize resources, learning to edit the unessentials, learning how to set and evaluate goals, and rewarding yourself for accomplishments.

Managing money is a different story. It involves dividing your wants from your needs, keeping track of income and expenses, and living within your means, not the means of others, as in "keeping up with the Joneses." Money management means being disciplined. It means learning how to enjoy delayed gratification. It also means finding and enjoying the things in life that are free.

Are time and money, or the lack of each, a stressor for you? What is one thing you could start right now to manage your time better? Are you the kind of person with champagne taste on a beer budget? What are some ways that you could gain a better handle on these two constraints to leisure and stress?

37. POETRY IN MOTION

"Yesterday is but a dream, tomorrow is only a vision,
But today well lived makes every yesterday a dream of happiness,
and every tomorrow a vision of hope.
Look well, therefore, to this day."
—Ancient Sanscrit Proverb

Prose is not the only style thought to be therapeutic for journal entries. Poetry is also highly suggested as a proven means to serve as an emotional catharsis. Although not all poems employ the element of rhyme, the use of rhyme in writing poetry allows the author the chance to make order out of chaos, thus giving a feeling or sense of control with perceptions of stressful events. In addition, the poetic license to use metaphors and similes from personal feelings allows a deeper sense of emotional expression. Many poets, including Emily Dickinson, Robert Frost, and Rod McEuen, have credited the use of poetry in their ability to gain a better perspective on expressing their feelings.

The healing process of self-expression through poetry, as described by M. R. Morrison in his book *Poetry as Therapy*, incorporates imagination, intuition, and the development of personal insight, three characteristics essential in the healing process. In turn, these poem entries augment the self-awareness process as the poem is first written and subsequently read in its entirety. As with other journal entries, poems can address a whole host of issues and emotions. For this reason poetry therapy is currently used as a therapeutic tool in the treatment of emotional disorders and illness from hospitals to prisons. This writing method is encouraged as a complementary journal writing style. In the words of one anonymous philosopher, "Poetry is mass confusion understood."

Here's a chance to try your hand at poetry. Write a poem to express how you feel now. Perhaps the theme of your poem can be related to your life in general, or some specific aspect (e.g., relationships, nature, holidays, anger, fear, love, or anything) that seems to lay heavy on your mind. Remember, poems don't have to rhyme. You can write your poem any way you choose and about anything. Take a pen or pencil in hand and try to make some written order out of confusion that may harness your thoughts. You may be quite surprised at the results.

38. NO REGRETS

"Tomorrow doesn't matter, for I have lived today."
–Horace

How many times have you looked back on something you did or said and thought to yourself, "Gee, if only I had..." or "I should have done..." ? As the saying goes, "Hindsight is twenty-twenty!" Yet, for every action or behavior that we wish we had done differently, there are literally hundreds, if not thousands, of personal accomplishments we pass over as simple achievements or "things to be expected." Only when we look at this critical mass of lifelong experience do we realize that every experience, good or bad, is valuable, if we take the time to learn from it.

Rather than dwelling on the "should haves," which can result in unnecessary guilt trips, take a moment to look back on the things that you have done that make you proud, happy, or just plain amazed. Recall those experiences that, if you had to live over again, you would do them exactly the same way with no regrets whatsoever! Make a list of these memorable moments and jot down beside each what it was (the key factor) that made this episode memorable.

Many times, people on their death bed look back on their lives and give a sigh as they recite a litany of regrets: things never accomplished, and issues never resolved. There is a inspirational message attributed to a women named Nadine Starr who once said,

> If I had to do it over again, I would try to make more mistakes next time. I would relax. I would be sillier this trip. I would climb more mountains, swim more rivers, and watch more sunsets. If I had to do it over again, I would go places, do things, and travel lighter than I have. If I had my life to live over again, I would start barefoot in the spring and stay that way later in the fall. I would play hooky more. I would pick more daisies.

If you were to jump into the future for a moment and look back on your life, what events, what situations, and what experiences would you like to look back on as having done to complete satisfaction? Now, having pondered over this and having made a list of these things, pick one or two, perhaps even three, and make an action plan to do each one without the trace of regret. Remember one thing: balance the freedom of choice with the responsibility of actions so you have no regrets! Every now and then, return to this list and add to it, if necessary. Remember, every day is a new beginning; carpe diem—seize the day!

39. GUILT AND WORRY

The difference between a state of stress and a state of relaxation is simple. In a stressful frame of mind, we are occupied with events or issues from the past and/or the future. During a state of relaxation we can enjoy the present moment; we can absorb and appreciate life's simple pleasures. Stress robs us of the present moment.

As psychologist Wayne Dyer suggests in his best-selling book, *Your Erroneous Zones*, there are two human emotions employed exclusively in the stressful state of mind. They are guilt and worry. *Guilt* preoccupies the mind with events and feelings from the past, while *worry* attracts our attention to events that are or might be held in the future. What both of these emotional states or zones have in common is that they both immobilize our thought processes and leave us unable to function at our best. These emotions cloud the mind and freeze rational thought processes that are truly needed to deal with our stressors.

While events from our past may serve as excellent learning experiences, all the guilt in the world will not change what has already occurred. Likewise, worrying is unproductive thinking. Too much of it can wreak havoc with the body's internal organs. Worrying about the future, not to be confused with planning for the future, is an unproductive emotion. Worrying is an immobilizing emotion. It wastes a lot of time, and time is too valuable a resource to waste. Most, if not all, of our stressors produce an excess of either one or both of these emotions. Not only do they rob us of the ability to enjoy the present moment, but they also inhibit us to act in a way to resolve the issue that created these emotional responses.

Are you a chronic worrier? Are there specific items that you worry about, or do general concerns trigger your worry emotion? Make a list of your top ten stressors again. Take a good look at them. Do they promote guilt or worry? Many people feel uncomfortable in the present moment. They would rather focus their attention on past or future events to avoid the present moment. Are you one of these people? Self-imposed guilt trips are very stressful. Is this an occasional characteristic of yours? Do you lay an occasional guilt trip on others to manipulate their emotions and behavior? Why? What are some ways to cut down on the use of these two emotions in your strategy to deal effectively with stress?

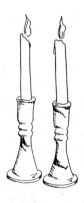

40. MOTHER EARTH

"Let us think of Mother Earth."
—Native American Prayer

It is no overstatement to say that the planet earth is in trouble! It is sick and desperately fighting for its survival. Water and air pollution, nuclear waste dumps, holes in the ozone, deforestation, and the incredible rate of extinction of plants and animals per day; the telltale signs are everywhere. All you need to do is listen to the news or read a magazine and these stories jump out and smack you across the face.

It may seem hard to believe that the earth is a living entity. Western thought, so heavily grounded in the scientific ideology, makes this idea seem pagan at best. But, if you were to listen to the Wisdom Keepers of the earth's indigenous tribes, you would find that this notion of the earth as a living entity is not foolish or ludicrous. It is a simple truth. Even the Ancient Greeks believed this, naming the mother earth, *Gaia*. Humans, once so close to the energies of the earth have now grown very distant and separate from them. From air conditioned bedrooms (carbofluorocarbons) to the automobile (carbon monoxide), we have become slaves to the benefits of technology. Still, it is not uncommon to hear people say that technology can fix what technology has damaged, in essence, putting human capabilities above the powers of the earth and sky. In the profound words of Chief Seattle, "All things connect. Man did not weave the web of life, he is merely a strand in it. Whatever he does to the web, he does to himself."

Sometimes in the cyclone of daily hassles and catastrophic events of our lives, we become disconnected from the natural elements that surround us. Whether or not we realize it, like a web, we are strongly connected to the earth. Despite all the wonderful advances in technology, we are still very dependent on the fruits and sustenance that the Mother Earth provides and the cycles in which she turns. *Stress* has recently been defined as that being separated or disconnected: disconnected from our friends, family and the earth that sustains us. Inner peace is synonymous with connection and harmony with all. Therefore, part of the strategy to reduce stress is to reconnect with the planet we call home. Perhaps it's true that we can't change the world, but we can change a part of it by our interaction with it. This idea is summed quite nicely in the slogan, "Think Globally, Act Locally."

Now is the time to do some soul searching with your Mother Earth in mind. If this concept is something you have never given serious thought to, now is the time to get serious, and not in a stressful way either. Here are some questions you can ask yourself to get the ball rolling:

1. How would you best describe your relationship with the planet earth?

2. Do you see the earth as a rock spinning in space, or as a living entity that provides sustenance in one form or another to all her species of flora and fauna?

3. Getting back to nature can take many forms, from gardening to exotic vacations. What do you do to get back to nature when the urge strikes?

4. Biological rhythms and circadian variations are constant reminders that the earth strongly influences us. Are you in touch with these rhythms and, if not, why?

5. Any good relationship takes work. If so inclined, what steps do you feel you can take to enhance your relationship with the Mother Earth?

41. FROM A DISTANCE

Sometimes when we distance ourselves from our problems, we tend to get a different and perhaps more objective viewpoint of the perceptions that we find ourselves having. Looking at ourselves through someone else's eyes gives us a chance to detach from our emotions long enough to find a new way to deal with the problem. When people write journal entries, they almost exclusively write in the first person (I). This first person viewpoint is often what separates autobiographical truth from a third person point of view, which is often incomplete because it lacks significant personal insight. But let us assume for a moment that an occasional journal entry could be written in the third person voice (she, he). Imagine what could be revealed using that unique insight only you could provide, but with the objectivity of a third person with no emotional attachment—the best of both worlds.

A journal entry of this nature would read like a story or screen play. It would have a plot (your stressor of the day), it would have character development (your thoughts and feelings this observer described), it would have mystery (how to resolve the stressor), and it might even have adventure and romance, but let's not get carried away. Save this journal entry when you have had a really bad day or your mind has been weighted down so heavily that you just cannot be objective with your thoughts, then pull out a pen, and as you write about this concern, give the slant of someone else looking at the situation. You'll be surprised at just how therapeutic, and revealing, this type of entry can be.

42. BEHAVIORS I'D LIKE TO CHANGE

"If one desires change, one must be that change first
before that change can take place."
—Gita Bellin

If you are like most people, you seek some type of self-improvement on a regular basis. Perhaps it's something you notice yourself doing. More likely, it may be a friendly suggestion from a friend, or worse, someone you aren't too particularly fond of. The most recognized time to make behavioral changes is January 1st, when the year is new, the slate is clean, and the winds of change are in the air. Another time that we are reminded to make changes is on or around our birthdays, again a clean slate.

Two types of personalities and the respective behaviors linked with stress have now become household words: Type A and Co-dependent. Type A behaviors include compulsive actions related to time urgency, super competitiveness, and hostile aggression. These characteristics, primarily feelings of unresolved hostility, are thought to be closely associated with coronary heart disease. Co-dependent behaviors include perfectionism, super over-achievement, ardent approval seeking, control of others, inability to express anger and other feelings, ardent loyalty to loved ones, and over-reactionaries. These types of behavior are now strongly linked to cancer.

Sometimes we are aware of our behaviors, but many times we are not. Specific actions can become so ingrained into our being that they become second nature and we seldom give them a second thought. It is only at those times when something we do is pointed out to us, or in an unguarded moment, that we see ourselves as perhaps others see us.

Behavioral psychologists have come to agree that changes are made first through awareness and then through motivation to change. But changing several habits at one time, which usually people try to do at the start of each new year, is very difficult, if not impossible. What is now commonly suggested is to try to change one behavior at a time. This way there is a greater chance of accomplishment. There is a progression of steps that, when taken, augment this behavior change process.

1. Become aware of your current behavior (i.e., biting your fingernails).

2. Think of a new mind frame to precede the new behavior you want to introduce (biting my nails is bad and I need to stop doing this).

3. Substitute a new and more desirable behavior in place of the old one (in the act of biting nails, stop and take a few deep breaths to relax).

4. Reevaluate the outcome of trying the new behavior and see what you think (breathing helped, especially on that date last night, let's keep trying this).

Sometimes it helps to write it down. Do you have any behaviors that you wish to modify or change? What are your options? Sketch them out here!

43. LOVE

"Love means letting go of fear."
—Gerald Jampolski

Love. It seems that no other concept has puzzled humankind so much as this single word. It is love that gives life and paradoxically people lose their lives in the name of love. As a professor who studied, taught, and has written several books on the subject, Dr. Leo Buscaglia admits that to define love is virtually impossible. Impossible it may be, but like the elusive Holy Grail, people continue to try to describe this abstract concept as they best know how. Among authors, poets, songwriters, and actors, the vehicles of love's message are endless.

After years of research, Buscaglia offered his own incomplete definition, suggesting that love is that which brings you back to your real self. In Buscaglia's book entitled *LOVE*, he writes, "For love and the self are one and the discovery of either is the realization of both." Just as charity is said to begin at home, so too must love reside within the individual before it can be shared. Buscaglia suggests that to share love, you must first give yourself permission to posses and nurture this quality within yourself. Furthermore, self-love begins with self-acceptance, unconditional self-acceptance.

It is interesting to note that the psychology field has pretty much ignored this emotion during the twentieth century, instead giving the limelight to anxiety and fear. Because of sexual connotations, love as an inner resource has been virtually disregarded much to the detriment of all human society. More recently, through the work of Buscaglia, Kubler–Ross, Siegel, Borysenko and others, this aspect of the human condition is being given more serious attention. In the much acclaimed book, *The Road Less Traveled*, psychiatrist M. S. Peck offers his own insights about the concept of love. From empirical observations, Peck perceived that there are many echelons of love: sharing, caring, trust, passion and compassion, with the highest level of love being a divine essence he calls *grace*.

Let there be no doubt, love is a profound concept. It is a value, an emotion, a virtue, a spiritual essence, an energy, and, to many people, an enigma. Love can inflict emotional pain just as it can heal the scars and bruises of the soul. It can make a fool out of the bravest man and a hero out of an underdog. Likewise, the expression of love can be quite intimidating as well; and in the American society, as a rule, love is often extended with conditions. Ultimately, it is these strings that taint our perception of love, whereas unconditional love may be the ultimate expression of grace. When people hear the word love, visions of Hollywood silver screen passion often come to mind. We have been socialized to think that love has to be as dynamic as Superman, yet the power of love can be as subtle as a smile or a happy thought.

If you were to make an attempt to define love, how would you begin to describe your interpretation of this concept? Is your expression of love limited by your level of self–acceptance? In your expression of love to others do you find that you attach conditions with it? In your opinion, how does falling in love differ from unconditional love? Add any thoughts to your definition of love here as well.

44. LESSONS LEARNED

Is it possible that life is one big schoolroom or that the planet earth is a laboratory for learning? There are many people who believe so. But unlike the structural classrooms that we attend from kindergarten through graduate school, the classroom of life is virtually experimental in nature. Moreover, there are neither grades nor curves. There are no diplomas, just a wealth of accumulated knowledge that we call *wisdom*.

The school of life does not require studying in the form of memorization as much as it does necessitate a continual synthesis of information and experiences that we come upon. The premise of our individual lesson plans is to discover the universal truths and to apply these in the framework of our lives. Each experience we encounter has a lesson to offer if we so choose to take the time to learn from it. As with other forms of schooling, there are those times when we play hooky and miss out on important material. In the end, our lives are an open book in which we write our lessons learned within the pages.

Some of life's lessons are so obvious that we walk right through, missing them completely. Others are so painful that we choose to avoid them. However, through it all we are very much aware, either consciously or unconsciously, of the meaning of our experiences. There is an ancient Chinese proverb that states, "when the pupil is ready, the teacher will come," meaning that when we take the time to explore the purpose of our life experiences, the lessons will be learned. To be "ready"is to be still with thought, allowing the mind liberty to interpret the meaning of these lessons.

Before you start this journal theme, you might want to sit comfortably, close your eyes for a moment and relax. Take a few deep breaths and begin to clear your mind of any distracting thoughts. Then use the following questions to ready the student within yourself so that the teacher may come.

1. What would you say is the most valuable lesson(s) that you have learned in your life to date?
2. What events led to this experience?
3. What was it that sparked this moment of revelation?
4. Are there any experiences that you still question the meaning of?
5. What events that have caused you pain which you are avoiding, may ultimately bear the fruit of understanding once resolved?
6. Finally, there is an expression that says, "To know and not to do, is not to know." Are there some lessons you have learned and hence forgotten to apply in your life that cause history to repeat itself? If so, what are they? Do you have any additional comments you wish to add?

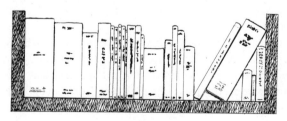

45. SELF-ESTEEM
The Bottom Line

Many themes in this journal workbook revolve around the concept of self-esteem. Self-esteem is considered by many to be the bottom line with regard to the perceptions of stressors and, indeed, how we manage our stress. *Self-esteem* is often defined as our personal level of self-approval. It is used synonymously with self-worth, self-respect, and self-value. Ultimately, strong self-esteem equates to the degree of acceptance and love we bestow upon ourselves. High self-esteem can sometimes be mistaken and confused with over-confidence, cockiness, and aggressiveness. So, in a humble effort we tend to compensate. Often, the result is modesty to the point of negativism, and negativism perpetuates low self-esteem. Today, there are many mixed messages that society gives which values both humbleness and greatness. It's a fine line drawn and straddled. We must learn to walk in balance.

Self-esteem is a complex concept. It includes, but is not limited to, self-understanding, acceptance, love, forgiveness, personal value system, and atonement. Self-esteem is as hard to measure as it is to define. Suffice to say that each of us knows generally where our self-esteem is as well as daily fluctuations and things that inflate or deflate it. Most everything we say, think, feel and do is a function of our self-esteem. In turn, messages that we communicate to ourselves and others from our thoughts, feelings and actions can reinforce either low or high self-esteem. When our self-esteem is low, like a bull's eye target, we become more susceptible to life's pressures. Conversely, when we are feeling good about ourselves, problems tend to roll off our backs quite easily. Stress becomes manageable, or simply dismissed altogether. There are four factors that contribute to strong self-esteem:

1. **Uniqueness**: Characteristics that make you feel special and unique.
2. **Power**: Feelings of self-reliance and self-efficacy, a "can do" attitude.
3. **Modeling**: Having a mentor or role model to identify with as a guide on your own personal life journey.
4. **Connectiveness**: Feelings of bonding and belonging with others, your network of friends and support groups.

The self-esteem concept, referred indirectly in previous journal themes, merits its own theme to write about. Take a moment to contemplate the idea of self-esteem, what your threshold is, and the bounds in which it oscillates. What are some ways to increase your threshold for a higher level of self-esteem? Do you see a relationship between your current self-esteem threshold and how well you deal with stress? Try to identify the following: five characteristics that make you unique, five factors that give you a sense of empowerment, five role models or mentors, and five friends or groups of people you consider to be part of your support system or connectedness.

46. FRIENDS IN NEED

"And let there be no purpose in friendship, save the deepening of the spirit."
—Kahlil Gibran, The Prophet

What is a friend? Perhaps it's someone to share the precious moments of life. Perhaps a friend is a confidant for our innermost thoughts and feelings. Most likely, a friend is someone just to be there, at times when we are in need of a helping hand or a comforting hug. Friends are all this and more. We as human beings are social by nature. Although there are times when being alone can serve as a great way to energize the soul, it is to our advantage to balance these times with the interactions and exchanges of those people whom we feel closest to, our network of friends.

Some interesting findings have emerged from research investigating the health and longevity of the world's oldest living citizens. We now know that involvement with friends who make up our social support group are as important to our health as regular exercise, proper nutrition, and sleep. It seems that in troubled times our friends can help buffer or neutralize the stress and tension that we feel is placed upon us. The bottom line is that the collection of friends we call our support group can help serve as an effective means to cope with stress.

As we grow and mature in our own lives, so do the relationships with our friends. The bonds we have with some people continually strengthen over time and distance while others seem to fray or fade. We often attract people into our lives with similar interests and ambitions. In some cases, our closest friends can seem more like family than our own brothers and sisters. In every case, friendships, like house plants and pets need attention and nurturing. Every now and then, it is a good idea to take a moment to evaluate our friendships, to see if they are truly fulfilling our needs. This inventory of friends can let us know if we have outgrown or grown apart from some people and the reasons why. It can also make us aware of the qualities that comprise a good, close, or best friend, as well as the difference between a good friend and an acquaintance. We also need to evaluate if we ourselves are making an equal contribution to each relationship. Here are some questions to help you with this assessment.

1. How would you best define the word *friend*, and what does being a friend mean to you?

2. What is it that draws a person into your life to become a friend?

3. Make a list of all your current friends. Are any members of your family in this group? How has this list changed over the past five years?

4. How would you evaluate your current circle of friends? Do you have several acquaintances that you call your friends?

5. Does your support group consist of people in different social circles, or is your's a closed circle of friends? Why would friends in different circles be of value?

6. What is it that keeps your bonds of friendships strong and what is it that tends to let some friendships fade away?

7. Are there any additional comments you wish to add here?

47. REFLECTIONS
Your Journal Summary

Every now and then it is a good idea to look back and see where you have traveled. A reflection on the past often gives us insight into how to best deal with the future. In this case, this reflection is a personal historical perspective, highlighting patterns and behaviors of our life, and as the saying goes, 'Those who fail to learn history's lessons, are bound to repeat them."

Often, we see our lives on a day-to-day basis. This is how the mind works best. However, like the study of history, we can learn much about ourselves by reviewing our past thoughts, attitudes, perceptions, and behaviors. Many times, patterns begin to emerge that are impossible to detect on a day-to-day basis. Patterns once uncovered or made aware of can either help us deal with our stressors or perpetuate our thought process, which in turn feeds the whole process of stress. By observing these patterns, awareness increases, and strategies can be planned to make our lives a little easier.

Now it is time to review your journal and see what lessons there are to be learned from your travels. Reread your journal entries, particularly the days when you just wrote what was on your mind. Then look for patterns or habits that stand out, those that perhaps you didn't know were part of your makeup or personality. Then begin to summarize what you have learned about yourself from rereading your journal entries. Rereading journal entries is like looking at old photographs. Some shots may not be too flattering, while others are going to bring back some great memories. You may also wish to include how rereading your thoughts and feelings might give you insight with how to help chart the next passage of your life journey until it comes time to reread it again. The question to be asked from this summary is, "What have I learned about myself from rereading these journal entries and how can I use what have I learned to help me down the road as I travel onward ?"

49

REFERENCES

Beattie, M., *Codependent No More,* Hazelton/Harper Press, New York, 1987.

Beattie, M., *Beyond Codependence,* Hazelton/Harper Press, New York, 1989.

Black Elk, W., and Lyons, W., *Black Elk ,* Harper, San Francisco, 1990.

Borysenko, J., *Minding the Body, Mending the Mind,* Bantam Books, New York, 1984.

Boyd, D., *Rolling Thunder,* Delta, New York, 1974.

Buscaglia, L., *Love,* Fawcett Crest, New York, 1972.

Buscaglia, L., *Living, Loving and Learning,* Fawcett Books, New York, 1982.

Casey, K. and Vanceburg, M., *The Promise of a New Day,* HarperCollins Publishers, New York, 1983.

Catacchione, L., *The Creative Journal, The Art of Finding Yourself,* Swallow Press, Athens, GA, 1979.

Dyer, W., *Your Erroneous Zones,* Avon Books, New York, 1976.

Fanning, P., *Visualization for Change,* New Harbinger Publication, Oakland, CA, 1988.

Foster, S., *The Book of the Vision Quest, by Steven* with Meredith Little, Prentice Hall Press, New York, 1988.

Frankl, V., *Man's Search for Meaning,* Pocket Books, New York, 1984.

Jampolski, *Love is Letting Go of Fear,* Celestial Arts, Berkeley, CA, 1979.

Jung, C.G., *Man and His Symbols ,* Anchor Press, New York, 1964.

Jung, C.G., *Mandalas of Symbolism,* Princeton University Press, Princeton, NJ, 1973.

Klein, A., *The Healing Power of Humor,* J.P. Tarcher, Los Angeles, 1989.

Kubler-Ross, E., *Death, The Final Stage of Growth,* Touchstone Books, New York, 1987.

Lerner, H., *The Dance of Anger,* Harper and Row, New York, 1985.

Lindbergh, A.M., *Gift from the Sea,* Vintage Books, New York, 1978.

Martz, H., *If I Had to Live my Life Over Again, I would pick more Daisies,* Paper Mache´ Press, Watsonville, CA, 1993.

McCaa, E. (Eagleman) *Mother Earth Spirituality,* Harper Collins, San Francisco, 1990.

Peter, L. and Dana, B., *The Laughter Prescription,* Ballantine Press, New York, 1982.

Peck, M.S., *The Road Less Traveled,* Touchstone Press, New York, 1978.

Peck, M.S., *The Different Drum,* Touchstone Books, New York, 1987.

Sanford, J., *Dreams and Healing,* Paulist Press, New York, 1978.

Seattle, Chief, A Letter from Chief Seattle, 1855 (from Ed McCaa Eagleman,) *Mother Earth Spirituality,* Harper Collins, San Francisco, 1990.

Schaef, A.,W., *Co-Dependence; Misunderstood, Mistreated,* Harper and Row, New York, 1986.

Siegel, B., *Love, Medicine & Miracles,* Perennial Press, New York, 1987.

Siegel, B., *Peace, Love, & Healing,* Perennial Press, New York, 1990.

Simonton, O.C., Simonton, S., and Creighton, J., *Getting Well Again,* Bantam Books, New York, 1978.

von Oech, R., *A Whack on the Side of the Head,* Warner Books, New York, 1983.

von Oech, R., *A Kick in the Seat of the Pants,* Perennial Library, New York, 1986.

Weisinger H., *The Anger Workout Book,* Quill Books, Harlinton, TX, 1985.

JOURNAL WRITING

Additional Resources

Abbott, H.P., *Diary Fiction: Writing as Action.* Cornell University Press New York, 1984.

Abercrombie, B., *Keeping a Journal.* Margaret K. McKelderry Books, New York, 1987.

Adams, K., *Journal to the Self.* Warner Books, New York, 1990.

Baldwin, C., *One to One: Self-Understanding Through Journal Writing.* M.Evans, & Co., New York, 1977.

Britton, J., Burgess, T., Martin, N., McLeod, A., and Rosen, H., *The Development of Writing Abilities.* Macmillan Publishing, London, 1975.

Buzan, T., *Use Both Sides of Your Brain.* E.P. Dutton, Inc., New York, 1983.

Capacchione, L., *The Creative Journal: The Art of Finding Yourself.* Swallow Press. Athens, GA, 1979.

DeVota, Bernard (Ed.), *The Journals of Lewis and Clark.* Houghton Mifflin, Boston, 1953.

Dinesen, I., *Out of Africa,* Random House Inc., New York, 1983.

Foster, S., with Little, M., *The Book of the Vision Quest; Personal Transformations in the Wilderness.* Prentice–Hall Press, New York, 1988.

Fulwiler, T. (Ed.), *Journals Across the Disciplines.* Northeast Regional Exchange, Inc. Chelmsford, MA. 1985.

Goldberg, N., *Writing Down the Bones.* Shambhala Publications, Inc., Boston, 1986.

Hagan, K.L., *Internal Affairs: A Journal Keeping Workbook for Self-Intimacy.* Escapadia Press, Atlanta, 1988.

Holly, M.L., *Writing To Grow: Keeping a Personal Profession Journal.* Heinemann Educational Books, NH, 1989.

Kaiser, R. B., The Way of the Journal. *Psychology Today,* 15:64–65, 1981.

Leedy, J.L., *Poetry Therapy: The Use of Poetry in the Treatment of Emotional Disorders.* J. B. Lippincott Co., Philadelphia, 1969.

Mallon, T., *A Book of One's Own: People and Their Diaries.* Ticknor and Fields, New York, 1984.

Mayer, H., Lester, N., and Pradl, G., *Learning to Write, Writing to Learn.* Boynton/Cook Publishers, Inc., Portsmouth, NH, 1983.

Morrison, M.R., *Poetry as Therapy.* Human Sciences Press Inc., New York, 1987.

Pennebaker, J. W., *Opening Up: The Healing Power of Confiding in Others.* William Morrow and Co., New York, 1990.

Progoff, I., *At a Journal Workshop.* Dialogue House Library, New York, 1975.

Progoff, I., *The Practice of Process Meditation.* Dialogue House Library, New York, 1980.

Rainer, T., *The New Diary.* J.P. Tarcher, Los Angeles, 1978.

Rico, G.L., *Writing the Natural Way.* J.P. Tarcher, Los Angeles, 1983.

Seaward, B.L., *Managing Stress: Principles and Strategies for Health and Wellbeing.* Jones and Bartlett Publishers, Boston, MA, 1994.

Simons, G.F., *Keeping Your Personal Journal.* Ballantine/Epiphany, New York, 1978.

JOURNAL ENTRIES

The Gift of Light
Is here for all to see.
The Joy of Love
Gives light to those who need,
Contribute to the Light.
                    —BLS

ABOUT THE AUTHOR

Brian Luke Seaward is an assistant professor in the Department of Health and Fitness at The American University, Washington D.C., where he teaches courses in Stress Reduction, Health and Wellness, Behavioral Medicine, Humor and Health, and Exercise Physiology. Dr. Seaward received his B.A. in journalism from the University of Maine at Orono, his M.S. in exercise physiology from the University of Illinois at Champaign-Urbana, and his Ph.D. in Health Promotion and Wellness (an interdisciplinary program) from the University of Maryland in College Park. He is a certified Stress Management Educator through the Association for Applied Psychophysiology and Biofeedback. Dr. Seaward has been invited to speak on the topic of stress management and wellness to such organizations as IBM, AT&T, Kodak, The Olympic Biathlon Team, The American Cancer Society, The American Heart Association, The United States Postal Service, and The National Safety Council. When not instructing, consulting, or counseling stress management programs, Dr. Seaward relaxes back home in the Colorado Rocky Mountains.